YOUR MONEY
THEIR MINISTRY

YOUR MONEY THEIR MINISTRY

A Guide to Responsible Christian Giving

By
Edward J. Hales
and
J. Alan Youngren

WILLIAM B. EERDMANS PUBLISHING COMPANY
GRAND RAPIDS, MICHIGAN

Copyright © 1981 by Wm. B. Eerdmans Publishing Co.
255 Jefferson Ave. SE, Grand Rapids, Mich. 49503
Printed in the United States of America

Library of Congress Cataloging in Publication Data
Hales, Edward J., 1927-
Your money, their ministry.
1. Christian giving.   2. Investments.
3. Fund raising.   I. Youngren, J. Alan,
1937-   .   II. Title.
BV772.H178   248'.6   81-5541
ISBN 0-8028-1894-3   AACR2

CONTENTS

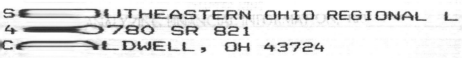

FOREWORD

Like all Christians, we readers of this book give money to advance God's work on earth. We are concerned about the results of those ministries to which we contribute, especially their success in bringing people to faith in Jesus Christ and changing their lives. We are less concerned about whether our contributions are used wisely, whether the institution or organization is managed well.

"My job is to give the money; the fund-raiser's job is to use it right," a capable businessman told me. "If he doesn't, that's between the Lord and him. It's not my responsibility." This attitude of blind trust, while seemingly Christian, provides the climate in which waste of resources, personal profiteering, and even fraud may flourish. But how can we know that our attempts at faithful stewardship are matched by faithfulness on the part of those who receive and administer the funds we contribute?

My friends Alan Youngren and Ed Hales have written this book to answer that question. All of us may profit from their considerable experience and careful research. By answering the questions publicly, Hales and Youngren have done their part to encourage fiscal accountability that is Christian. In doing so, they are in excellent company. Senator Mark Hatfield has been a leader in advancing public and Christian awareness of the need for such financial accountability.

Some works of God are local and therefore visible: churches, rescue missions, youth ministries. But others that receive immense sums of money in today's pattern of Christian giving — television programs, educational institutions, parachurch organizations — are distant and cannot be observed. It is the latter

that are attracting attention from government agencies, especially the Internal Revenue Service. And Senator Hatfield realizes that more than money is involved: the credibility of the
evangelical movement is at stake, along with the future of our
tax-free institutions.

This is no H. L. Mencken or Sinclair Lewis treatment of
the subject. It is sober, responsible, and positive. In conver-
sations I had with one of the authors while the book was taking
shape, he expressed godly sorrow over organizations and institutions that didn't measure up to Christian expectations.

God requires faithfulness in His servants, and holds them
accountable. Should we require less of those to whom we en-
trust our investments in His Kingdom?

JOSEPH BAYLY

ACKNOWLEDGMENTS

Although we have spent years gathering the information for this book, we began working on it in earnest in April 1978, when we conducted the first of our two surveys. A little over two years later our work was complete, and the courageous people at Eerdmans took over. During those two years many people gave us valuable assistance, generously offering us their time and knowledge. We wish to thank a number of those contributors here.

- Stephen Board, Executive Editor of *Eternity* magazine and friend of the thoughtful Christian donor, was stellar in his role of literary midwife: he read every chapter as it appeared, making numerous helpful comments.
- James Sire, author and editor, was an eleventh-hour savior, a good influence and provider of direction.

- Chapter Nine would not be Chapter Nine without the counsel of Donald Mortensen, Controller of Seattle Pacific University, and Robert Erickson, Vice President and Controller of Servicemaster Corporation.

- Chapter Six got invaluable help from the good offices of Edwin L. (Jack) Frizen, Executive Director of the Interdenominational Foreign Mission Association.

- We received vitally important assistance with the historical information in Chapter Three from friends, acquaintances, and people we had never met — people too numerous to mention individually, but deserving of sincere thanks.

- Finally, we were able to complete the second survey of parachurch organizations with the appropriate anonymity because Marilyn Novak lent us the protective guise of her personal stationery. Marilyn and her husband Karl are now enduring the consequences of this benevolence: they are "hot prospects" on thirty or more mailing lists. We don't know how we will ever make this up to them.

INTRODUCTION

It is important that we make a clear opening statement about this book's purpose—about what it is attempting to do and what it does not intend to do.

The concerns of the traditional stewardship apologetic are not at issue here. The traditional stewardship book is about the "why," the "how," and the "how much" of giving. When such a book talks about the "how" of giving, it explains giving "with joy," "with sacrifice," and "in secret." We are glad that such books have been written; we recommend several that we think are particularly good.

But our book deals with an entirely different matter. We are addressing the steward who has already answered the questions of "why," "how," and "how much"; we are addressing the giver as a wise *investor*. Certainly Christ's parable of the talents (in Matthew 25) stresses the importance of handling money judiciously. It shows that the steward is responsible for the money he is entrusted with—for how well it is used, and for the kind of spiritual return it brings.

Today this means avoiding the pitfalls of certain less-than-worthy organizations asking for money. It means giving with sense as well as with love. And that is what this book is for—to help you become a steward who gives both joyfully *and* thoughtfully.

Keep in mind that we are not suggesting that you must follow every last bit of our advice to be an effective giver. Although we think that everything we advocate is valuable, we also think that each of our suggestions can be individually helpful.

EDWARD J. HALES
J. ALAN YOUNGREN

• CHAPTER ONE •

THE IMPORTANCE OF WISE STEWARDSHIP

*"And whatever ye do, do it heartily,
as unto the Lord, and not unto men."*

Colossians 3:23

John Rolf has his own business. An intelligent, thoughtful person, John makes all of his business decisions — large or small — very carefully. He spent almost as much time selecting the pocket-size calculators for his employees as he did choosing a new mini-computer, because he wants every choice to be right. John is equally careful with his personal finances: he keeps accurate records, and even projects future expenses.

Mary, John's wife, is equally as careful in her management of their home. Whether she is shopping at the supermarket — calculating price-per-ounce comparisons as she goes — or using consumer research publications to effectively choose a major appliance, she spends her money wisely.

Because both John and Mary are committed Christians, they support the Lord's work generously. They participate enthusiastically in their local church, and give liberally to it. They also feel led to support numerous parachurch organizations.

Unfortunately, in this area of financial management, John and Mary are surprisingly careless. All year long they are contacted personally by representatives of various groups, and besieged by appeals through the mail, over the radio, and on television. But, rather than selecting a limited number of organizations to help, they respond to as many of the groups as possible — providing they appear to share the Christian beliefs and goals that John and Mary support.

Actually, the two of them know very little about most of

1

the groups they help. True, the Rolfs support Mary's cousin, who is a missionary to Zaire, and she sends them frequent, specific reports about her work. And they also get frequent reports from the local staff member of a national youth ministry that they support. A few other organizations send newsletters occasionally — depending on their ability to afford them. But with these few exceptions, John and Mary know next to nothing about most of the organizations that they support.

And, sad as it is to realize, we must make no mistake about it: some of the organizations today that seek money in the name of Jesus Christ are not above making thoroughly fraudulent statements about how they will use that money. It is further true that every purportedly Christian fund-raiser can get John and Mary's name and address and send them something in the mail, and radio and television appeals are almost equally inescapable. But, you ask, aren't these unscrupulous operators and modern methods of mass communication at least partly to blame for John and Mary's malpractice of stewardship? And is it really so regrettable that John and Mary choose to spend their stewardship dollars as they do? After all, how much money is actually involved?

Keeping in mind that the Rolfs' behavior mirrors that of literally hundreds of thousands of Christian stewards, consider this: if John and Mary Rolf earn an average income, and if they give the percentage that most committed Christians do, then the total sum of money involved is definitely significant.[1] It represents a sum larger than that needed to buy several pieces of new furniture or several rooms of new carpeting. And whoever bought a sofa by answering a letter in the mail? In fact, this amount is probably greater than the amount that the average family spends on its car(s). The irony is that people like the Rolfs know much more about the strengths and shortcomings of General Motors, Ford, and Chrysler than they do about the quality of the foreign mission they support.

At this point you might be willing to admit the significance

---

[1]The Gallup Organization's survey for *Christianity Today* indicates that over fifty percent of 31 million evangelicals in the United States "go beyond the tithe" in their giving.

of the total amount that the Rolfs give, but be unwilling to admit the significance of each individual gift. Yet we contend that these individual gifts *are* very significant; in fact, they are the focus of the two principal points of this book.

Two great problems (as well as many lesser ones) plague Christian stewardship today. The first we call "dilution of effect," a problem caused by the proliferation of small gifts. Interestingly, there is a logical reason for combatting this problem by giving fewer gifts that are more substantial. As Harold Seymour points out in his book, *Designs for Fund-Raising*, the average donor has the "mental room" to maintain an active interest in approximately six organizations. If we evangelical donors could restrain our "acceptances" to six, then we would be giving six *significant* gifts to organizations we knew well.

Unfortunately, it seems that we can hardly refuse any appeal for funds. The result is meager individual donations — in fact, the average donation to a Christian cause is under ten dollars. Tom Watson, Jr., author of a perceptive article called "The Art of Intelligent Giving,"[2] criticizes such unfocused giving. "Impulsively peeling off a dollar or two in response to every appeal that sounds good can spread a Christian's stewardship too thin," Watson claims. "Shotgun giving . . . fails to make a real impact." It also makes it virtually impossible for the donor to keep track of the multitudes of organizations he supports.

What many donors don't realize is that processing costs are multiplied many times by a proliferation of small gifts. The cost of processing a gift doesn't vary with the gift's size because the processing procedure is always the same: any gift must be entered on the books and deposited in the bank, and the donor must be sent a receipt. This means that the recipient organization pays as much to process a $10.00 gift as it pays to process a $100.00 gift. Consequently, processing takes ten times the bite out of ten $10.00 gifts than it does out of one $100.00 gift.

As important a problem as it is, however, small-gift proliferation must be ranked second to the greatest concern among those pleading for responsible and effective stewardship: the

[2]From *Moody Monthly*, March 1972, p. 20.

concern that the money not fall into the wrong hands. Apparently there are two main reasons why a substantial proportion of the Christian public does not realize how many wholly unworthy organizations are after their stewardship dollar—and getting it.

First is a widespread conviction—or at least a prevalent attitude—that what the recipient organizations do with the money is "between them and God." Billy Melvin, President of the National Association of Evangelicals, calls this attitude "a cop-out,"[3] and we agree. Many people take this position—which absolves them from responsibility—because they covet the pleasurable emotional "trip" of believing in and saying "yes" to a wildly emotional fund appeal. The late A. W. Tozer, well-known pastor and writer from a denomination with particularly strong ties to missions (the Christian and Missionary Alliance), cautioned Christians to give "generously, but wisely." He went on to assert strongly that the "tender-hearted saints think with their feeling and pour out consecrated wealth indiscriminately on projects wholly unworthy of their support."

Supporting Tozer's conclusion are several studies which show that giving is eighty percent emotion, and only twenty percent deliberate evaluation of alternatives. Robert Sharpe, a nationally known consultant in the area of development, has made an even bleaker assessment of donors. Through extensive experience he has discovered and labeled the four basic kinds of donors: the impulsive, the habitual, the thoughtful, and the careful. Sharpe maintains that seventy percent of all donors are impulsive, and twenty percent are habitual; only seven percent are thoughtful givers, and a mere three percent are careful givers. Small wonder, then, that many unworthy organizations are being supported.

The second cause of careless giving is naivete: apparently many Christian donors fail to comprehend that some who seek the stewardship dollar are after personal gain. The leaders of the Mennonites have printed a particularly well-written brochure for their people entitled "Giving—From the Heart, with

---

[3]Quoted from his article "The Scandal of Evangelical Giving" in *United Evangelical ACTION*, Winter 1976, p. 12.

the Head."4 These well-informed leaders explain the problem with useful bluntness: "Some North American promoters of mission activity have amassed rather huge personal fortunes." Various other denominations and groups have made similarly blunt statements to alarm their people into listening to their warnings. Here is one of the sadder items from the Mennonites' record of misuse of funds:

> An agency that calls itself a "tax-exempt, non-profit missionary organization . . . to the communist world" boasted in its publicity that it had delivered by special airplane "in one day 160,000 copies of gospels and tracts to a communist country." To a Mennonite leader, a representative of that organization confided that the gospels and tracts had not actually been delivered inside the country, but had been sealed into plastic envelopes and dumped into the ocean, [in the hope] that they would float ashore.

Of course we can't react to this problem simply by cutting off all gifts to mission work behind the Iron Curtain — think of the effect on the several thoroughly legitimate foreign missions there. Yet we mustn't think that this is a highly unusual instance of corruption, either, because similar cases have been uncovered, as Melvin points out in his article. A few years ago, for example, a senate sub-committee investigated a child support agency with the word "Christian" in its name. They uncovered information — reported in the public press — that the agency had spent 2.4 million dollars of funds it had raised for charity to pay for advertising in order to raise still more money. Although it requested a special gift of $34.00 for each child, it delivered only $4.28 to the cause of helping the child and retained the rest.

Melvin goes on to explain that some organizations even perpetrate outright fraud:

> A mission in this country put pressure on an employee overseas to falsify the [record of the] amount of money sent from the USA to the overseas office. When the employee's Christian convictions would not permit him to is-

4This pamphlet, published in August 1973, is available from the Mennonite Board of Missions. A. W. Tozer's earlier-quoted comments appear here.

sue a receipt for several thousand dollars more than he had received, he had no option but to resign.

This kind of fraud sometimes involves abusing both people and things:

> On a trip overseas [Melvin] was asked about a certain organization in America which makes numerous appeals via radio, direct mail, and a magazine. A concerned Christian brother was troubled because a good friend, who was an employee of the organization, was being pressured to misrepresent facts, even to the point of taking pictures of public buildings and claiming they were orphanages supported by the group.

The essence of the problem for the God-fearing, effective organization is that unworthy organizations use the same methods of solicitation that it does — the media. In fact, the audience holding the stewardship dollars *seeks out* messages and appeals delivered through the media, because they are looking for ways to show Christian concern for others. Thus they read Christian magazines, listen to Christian radio programs, and watch Christian TV programs. And they end up on regular "need" mailing lists because of initial contributions that they make to various organizations.

Remember that every organization — worthy or otherwise — that vies for your money knows how to use effective fundraising techniques. They can *all* purchase a machine that automatically types you a "personal" letter, one that repeats your name at several strategic places. They can even buy a machine that will write in a signature. If this impersonal "personalization" bothers you, think of those most burdened by the media siege: those honest organizations that must battle the host of unscrupulous operators for your stewardship dollar. They refuse to use fraud and deception, as well as numerous questionable tactics. When they show this much integrity, how can we ask them not to mass-produce their appeal letters — especially when everyone else is doing it at substantial savings? Certainly the honest organization feels pressured to follow suit, to play the media "game."

In the gray area of right and wrong is the question of emphasis. Should an organization's messages emphasize the entire scope of its work, or should it continually push the "hot buttons"—child care, urgent building construction, and other effective emotional issues? Every organization knows that a picture of a sad-faced orphan is more effective than pictures of many other equally worthy causes, so it's tempting to use such a device to ensure a good response. One organization that we know of has perhaps yielded to this pressure. For years it consistently produced brochures with plainly expressed, substantive information about what it was doing in the field. Now, possibly in the face of financial difficulty, this organization has hired a fund-raiser away from a mission organization that is one of the "louder" and more successful of the current number, and their most recent piece featured—for the first time—the sad face of an orphan.

Certainly we can't say that this organization has necessarily used a misleading emphasis, nor can we say that such a picture is always used in a shrewdly calculated way. And we must understand the dilemma of the fund-raisers of the honest organizations. These individuals realize that getting money from people *is* a business, and they are sorely tried to go on believing that what the audience needs is solid, unspectacular information about what the ministry is doing—especially in the face of the success of emotional appeals that are often marginally relevant to primary causes.

Yet it is these very people—the organizations doing the effective work—to whom God would have us send our money. Given that the "tactics" of both the worthy and the unworthy organization are often similar, what should we do when confronted with "personal" letters, emotionally-charged brochures and films, powerful oration, and the rest of the arsenal of "the game"? How can we give the advantage in the game to the real works of God?

How? By following the lead of intelligent foundations, prudent church missions boards, and truly wise personal stewards—by seizing the initiative, by seeking out information and evaluating it. We need to find out all we want to know, not only what organizations may want to tell us.

The primary purpose of this book is to show that responsible stewardship does not lie in patiently hearing out every appeal. And the responsible and effective steward does not sit back and wait for the fund-raiser's advance. Instead, he takes the offensive, he secures the information he needs rather than the appeal that is pressed on him. He then uses this information — or the refusal to provide it — in a careful evaluation (outlined in detail later in this book). If he makes the decision to support an organization, his responsibility does not end with his initial investigation of it. If he is to continue to support it in a responsible way, he must continually evaluate its work, and make sure that he gets the necessary information to do so. (Getting such information from a reputable organization should not be that difficult. Reacting to the public's growing desire to know, honest organizations are increasingly willing to supply data that is quite complete — especially thorough financial data, as Chapters 7 and 9 explain. This trend is putting unworthy organizations in an increasingly precarious position.)

We have many hopes about what this book may accomplish, but our fondest hope is that God will use it to divert a substantial portion of the Christian stewardship dollars now flowing to organizations that — for a variety of reasons we discuss — are not getting the job done. We hope that he will make this money flow instead to those organizations that can use it honestly and fruitfully in their ministries. When more stewards have the information they need to give wisely, this can happen.

This book is also intended to help donors break the habit of giving numerous small gifts. Instead of the "scatter approach" to giving, we recommend goal-setting, information gathering, and evaluation, and advocate that the donor limit his support (beyond his own church) to six to ten organizations. With this approach, his rewards are many: he gets to know his recipients, they probably get to know him, and he will have a greater overall effect as a steward.

When we talk about limiting our gifts, an important and inevitable question arises: where does the local church fit into this picture? Outside the context of this book, our answer to that question would be different. Here, our answer is affected by our emphasis on the responsibility of the individual steward, and so is two-fold. First, the Christian as steward must necessarily see his church as one of the numerous candidates for his gifts. But, secondly, if he takes our advice, he will see that his church is first among the many, because we believe that the Bible indicates that the believer's church has first rights to his material support.

Beyond the biblical imperative are several other reasons for determining support for your local church "off the top." First, your church is the organization in which you have the greatest participatory role. You can join in its many activities of ministry, evaluate its work, and, as a voting member of the congregation, influence changes in its structure and procedure. Secondly, your church is supposed to be — and very often is — the center of your personal outreach, and it's appropriate that you support your own spiritual work. Finally, remember that the success of the local church is essential to the well-being of all mission efforts. Because it teaches Christian stewardship and nurtures good stewardship habits, the local church has been able to consistently supply Christian mission enterprises with both money and personnel. Naturally, the closer a steward is to his local church, the more he will give to it. Most Christians will support every aspect of their church's program. Others, while possibly doubtful of activities included in their church's missions budget, will nevertheless be thoroughly supportive of the congregation itself and eager to contribute to its financial support. There is no third category here — and there shouldn't be — because any committed Christian who cannot conscientiously support his church financially should not support that church with his attendance, either. He should find a church in which he can become a fully participative member.

In short, a good steward's first concern is his local church, but he is led to give beyond its bounds as he learns about need and opportunity elsewhere. In the following chapters we will discuss how the concerned steward can control both the quantity and the quality of these gifts.

• CHAPTER TWO •

WHY CHRISTIAN FUND-RAISING
HAS SKYROCKETED:
A Brief History of Fund-Raising in the Church *

Let's assume that you feel led to support God's work beyond your local church. When you think about other possible recipients for your gifts, you're amazed by the large number of groups that solicit your help: evangelical groups, other religious groups, secular charities, and educational institutions. How did so many groups ever discover that you exist? you ask yourself. How did they get your name and address? And why do they all think that you'll be interested in supporting them?

All groups use essentially the same "tactics," but for the purposes of this book we will concentrate on the how and why of evangelical fund-raisers. At this point you may be wondering why religious fund-raising is so prevalent today. This is a development you can better understand if you look at past history.

You should realize that, from the earliest ages, the raising of funds or resources has been part of the work of God. In fact, the Israelites made a major fund-raising effort (the first on biblical record) to maintain the Tabernacle in the wilderness: as they prepared to enter the Promised Land, God instructed them to support the priestly tribe of Levi "in return for the service they perform, the service of the Tent of meetings" (Num. 18:21). The people held a second major fund-raising event for the building of the Temple; and, according to I Chronicles 29,

---

*Two books in particular gave us valuable help on this subject: *Money and the Church* by Luther P. Powell (New York: Association Press, 1962), and *Modern Christian Movements* by John T. McNeill (Philadelphia: Westminster Press, 1957).

King David developed a funding campaign in which he employed techniques still used today by fund-raising consultants. (These forms of giving became traditional, which explains the rebuke of Malachi — who prophesied near the end of the Old Testament era — when the people withheld tithes and contributions.)

Jesus' ministry was also dependent on the support of his followers, as we discover in a remarkable text (Luke 8:1-3):

> And it came about soon afterwards that he began going about from one city and village to another, proclaiming and preaching the Kingdom of God, and the twelve were with Him, and also some women who had been healed of evil spirits and sicknesses: Mary who was called Magdalene, from whom seven demons had gone out, and Joanna, the wife of Chuza, Herod's steward, and Susanna, and many others who were contributing to their support out of their private means.

Even these few examples make it obvious that the securing of funds to meet the needs of the ministry is a legitimate part of God's work, and has been through all the ages of the church. Nevertheless, we can't help but feel that the tremendous quantity and intensity of appeals from evangelical groups today is excessive; we even wonder if certain groups are abusing their privilege of solicitation. This in turn makes us wonder about the integrity of church fund-raising since Pentecost. Were there abuses in the early days, too?

You can answer this question by remembering the Middle Ages, when a church-backed theology of merit by works paved the way for the sale of spiritual worth, the sale of escape from punishment for sin (indulgences), and even the sale of church office (simony). How are these medieval abuses related to today's barrage of fund appeals? One surprisingly strong factor links these two phenomena: the unwillingness of the laity to give in proportion to the church's size and resources — an unwillingness that fosters these shrewder methods of garnering funds. Actually, throughout most of the centuries of church history, the laity have failed to sustain the church's activity at the level that the clergy and other leaders deemed appropriate.

Consequently, the church in every century developed its own means of increasing the influx of funds, or of coping with limited resources in some other way. These methods were perhaps desperate and sometimes questionable, but they usually developed from good intentions — as do many of the pleas of evangelical groups today.

The medieval popes forced the money out of the laity by a variety of means, the Methodist circuit riders lived in poverty, and early American churches sold pew space and held lotteries. Whatever the circumstances, they all point to a phenomenon that developed when Constantine ended the stigma of belonging: when church membership involves little or no personal cost, the people place little value on that membership — and their giving shows it.

In the first and second centuries things were different: when belonging to the Body of Christ often meant persecution and death, the people gave freely and generously. They gave according to the principle of firstfruits, which meant giving the first portion of one's income (no hint was made then about the *proportion* of income each person should give). But by the fourth century church leaders found it necessary to insist on the tithe, because firstfruits were no longer forthcoming from any substantial portion of the faithful. And by the sixth century the tithe was Roman church law, upheld in church courts and enforced by threats as serious as excommunication.[1]

In 590, Gregory the Great ascended the throne of St. Peter, consolidating and tremendously extending papal power. What followed in the next 900 years was really less a matter of fundraising abuse than of the papacy becoming a nation state with the Pope its king (this was the case before and during the period of the rise of nation states, during the Middle Ages, and later). The Pope needed substantial resources to compete politically with kings and other leaders in an age when every common man needed to know who his physical protector was. The kings

[1]These laws were set down at the Second Council of Mascon, 585 A.D.

had subjects; the Pope had communicants who were much more like subjects than a flock of followers. And the fund-raising procedures of the papacy, based on a medieval theology of works and merit — and on the sale of that merit and of church office — were highly complex, enforced by law, and very successful.

You might think that the Reformation would have changed all this, that the Reformation principles of personal freedom and voluntary allegiance would have affected Protestant attitudes toward church support. Instead, the Luthers, Calvins, and Zwinglis were all convinced of the *unwillingness* of the laity to voluntarily supply sufficient funds to the church. And all over post-Reformation Europe church and state combined powers to raise church funds through tithing laws and outright state support. In fact, advocates of voluntarism in seventeenth-century Europe — the Anabaptists, the Quakers, the Separatists — were social outcasts, often politically persecuted.

Many of the principles of religious liberty that these groups stood for became goals of those who founded the first American colonies. But the question of church support itself, as a religious or political issue, failed to find a dominant role in the New World; and when members of these groups came to America they discovered that, as advocates of voluntary support, they were a minority within groups of colonial founders that had other goals and desires. The few groups that did support voluntarism lacked the clout to foster its growth. For example, both the Plymouth Colony Founders (the Pilgrims) and the Massachusetts Bay Founders (the Puritans) favored voluntarism; nevertheless, when the four commonwealths of Massachusetts, Plymouth, Connecticut, and New Haven united in 1643, one of their first governmental acts was to enact a law of church support.

The student of church history observes this continuing phenomenon: church leaders, dissatisfied with the laity's level of commitment, held to the necessity of compulsory church support, which in turn fostered further unwillingness to give — and so the classic vicious circle continued. Besides creating financial burdens, compulsory church support laws alienated the people from their church and its leaders, especially when the clergy used the laws to take people to court. And the church in America learned another painful truth as it struggled to put aside unbiblical means of raising funds—namely, that the absence of compulsory support is no guarantee of the presence of New Testament voluntarism.

Voluntarism made a kind of comeback when American churches were impressed by notable attempts at voluntary fund-raising by other Christian outreach efforts, and by the end of the eighteenth century the churches had shed most compulsory support laws. Yet what replaced these laws only ushered in a new era in the struggle for voluntarism, because the clergy and lay leadership, fearing the laity's unwillingness to give as much as ever, developed an extensive repertoire of "procedures" as safeguards. These procedures (probably too dignified a word for them) were designed to "ease" the support out of the people rather than forcing it out of them, as before. Most notable among these procedures were the following:

1. Pew space was sold or rented, or each family in the church was assessed a "pew fee." The best locations in the church cost the most, and there was a section in the rear reserved for the poor, or any in the church who didn't want to pay for a pew—in effect, any who could bear the stigma of sitting back there. This practice was extremely widespread, even though it usually didn't raise enough money and created social disharmony by discouraging visitors and encouraging class consciousness and ill will in the congregation.

2. Lotteries were commonly held. Sometimes participation was limited to the congregation, but more often anyone could buy chances. The lottery developed as a form of entertainment during the time of the caesars; it was first used to raise money in fifteenth-century Europe. According to records, the first lottery in America took place in 1720, and for the next century the lottery was dignified by the participation of our nation's most respected leaders. It was further dignified by its important role in church fund-raising, which began in 1749, when the Trenton Presbyterian Church held the first American church lottery. The churches clung to this means of income even after

public sentiment turned against it; proof is in the record of New Jersey churches, which took lotteries to other states when their own state legislature ruled against the games.

3. Subscription lists were the natural successor to outright taxation and the forerunner of the pledge system. These lists, though seldom seen today, are still in use nevertheless. The lists were circulated to everyone in the congregation, so of course social pressure was hard at work, because each member could see what others had given. Often the list was "baited" at the top with the names of the most generous supporters, and the amounts they gave. And sometimes church officers even went to the extreme of indicating what each party "ought" to give.

4. The glebe — owned by the church — was land the preacher farmed to supplement his income. Technically, parishioners didn't have to help farm that land — but they knew they wouldn't see much of their pastor if they didn't. This was a clever way of getting the average parishioner to invest valuable man-hours in his preacher's livelihood.

5. Buying and selling in the church seems an obvious flouting of the biblical message of Jesus driving the moneychangers from the temple — but American churches have sold everything from books[2] to insurance. They have also tried any number of other ventures to raise income — held pie raffles, bought real estate, built offices to rent. Of all the "procedures" listed, this one is by far the most popular today.

The American church's primary dependence on voluntarism today is not the result of a gradual shift in emphasis: the church was pressured by movements and institutions outside itself to change. These groups (truly parachurch groups) were often comprised of a much larger proportion of committed believers than was the church as a whole. As a result, they found voluntarism an easy and natural means of raising funds.

The first of these groups were all part of The Great Awakening, the tremendous revival of biblical Christianity that swept

[2]Church book-selling is often a service to the congregation and no more — but sometimes it goes beyond that.

through most of Europe, the British Isles, and America during the last half of the eighteenth century and the first half of the nineteenth century. At its core were the preaching and work of Jonathan Edwards, George Whitefield, the Wesleys, and literally scores of other important evangelical leaders. These men were not about to wait for the established church to experience a revival so that the Awakening could work through the traditional machinery. They believed instead in organizing around the activity — the work God was doing.

Methodism was one belief system that grew out of the Awakening. (Though John Wesley — the British founder of Methodism — tried long and hard to keep his ties with the Church of England, Methodism was outside that church from its inception.) Wesley divided his followers into cell groups called classes, and collected funds from them (in the days of early Methodism). These donations had to be substantial, because Wesley needed funds to act on the social concerns in which he and other Great Awakening leaders were interested. Out of this the Clapham Sect developed, a group made up largely of wealthy evangelical Anglican businessmen who were concerned about the needs of their fellowmen. Interestingly, Methodism was probably the single most important factor that influenced the church to adopt pure voluntarism.

Another highly important development of the Great Awakening was the rise of modern missions, which began with William Carey's work in India. This movement has drawn much of its impetus from "faith mission work," which depended on voluntary support from interested parties rather than on the resources of the established churches or (in earlier times) the governments of the European colonial powers.

Because of this continually growing influence of voluntaristic fund-raising, and the slow but sure forfeiture of the traditional fund-raising machinery by the established denominations, fund-gathering in the church had changed significantly by the mid-twentieth century. The church and a sizable list of parachurch organizations basically had only one acceptable way to solicit our support: by presenting their work to us — and making their needs known to us — convincingly.

But this is still not a fully up-to-date view; two additional phenomena have made their mark since the 1940s:

1. *Proliferation of Effort*

John Wesley built up Methodism outside of Anglicanism — reluctantly, but out of necessity. This development of the parachurch caught on, and undoubtedly God has used many parachurches to further his work. But in America, where the rugged individualist is the hero and the frontier mentality is often the ideal, the parachurch — with its implication of breaking new and challenging religious ground — is almost too popular. The same spirit that has prompted us to develop an almost unbelievable number of denominations also causes us to suffer from the "parachurch syndrome": when someone in a parachurch group doesn't like the way the leadership handles a particular decision — or simply doesn't like being a subordinate — he reacts by starting his own group. This perpetual splintering has greatly multiplied religious work and mission efforts.

The second great multiplier of these groups is sheer tenacity: once formed, these groups seldom "die." Few — if any — ever fully succumb because of lack of funds; they may shrink somewhat, but they almost never declare themselves inoperative, simply admitting that circumstances change and that they are no longer effective in their work. True, a fairly large number have radically altered their goals and the nature of their work to more accurately reflect their donors' interests. But many others are determined to limp on; in fact, in all of the rather extensive files we have accumulated over many years on the subject of Christian fund-raising, we find record of only one Christian ministry informing its supporters that it was ceasing operation.[3] We are not suggesting that only the "superpowers" of Christian fund-raising should survive; but we would like to see the voluntary demise of those groups receiving so little financial and spiritual support that they can't function effec-

---

[3]There have been mergers, however. The Interdenominational Foreign Mission Association reports ten mergers among its members during the past ten years.

tively. By stubbornly surviving they only drain off valuable support from more viable groups.

The world of advertising offers a helpful model to the world of religious fund-raising. No doubt Madison Avenue gives birth to more businesses than any other breeding ground like it: new agencies spring up literally every day. But because the law of the marketplace prevails, it assures a like number of failures — and closings. As buyers compare products and choose the best among them, quality prospers and mediocrity dwindles. It is a kind of survival of the fittest. If, in a similar way, donors to religious groups compared the "products" of these various organizations and decided to support only the most effective, the best would grow and do more of God's work, and the worst would disappear for lack of support. Currently, however, most donors are judging only by the fund-raisers' stories — each seemingly more compelling than the last.

2. Inflation: Worldwide and Rampant

In a world in which the businessman can't simply raise his prices when costs increase, he must have more money next year simply to repeat last year's performance. And Christian fund-raisers are certainly familiar with the problem — running hard just to stay in the same place. Workers for world missions find this problem compounded by the weakness of the dollar abroad. In foreign countries with a currency stronger than the dollar, each slip of the dollar magnifies the effects — for the mission organization — of domestic inflation. And in those nations with a currency rate weaker than the dollar, inflation is commonly double or triple the U.S. rate.

The problem of Christian ministries, then, is obvious: those in this country need an annual increase in dollars equal to the inflation rate just to continue their present level of effort, while those in foreign places need even more funds to do their work. Inevitably, the cry is "We need more money!" and the answer invariably is "Do more fund-raising! Reach more people more often!"

CHAPTER THREE

THE MODERN FUND-RAISER'S TOOLS:
The Media Arsenal

Given the perpetual pressure on organizations to continually increase their audience, the question is this: can every group find the tools to reach more people more often? Can every Christian fund-raiser buy another mailing list, broadcast to a larger audience, and take other promotional steps to get the additional monies that inflation and other pressures demand? Apparently they can — if they can find the money to pay for it — because Christian fund-raising activity has increased dramatically in this century. This activity has been matched by — and spurred on by — the equally rapid advances in fund-raising technology. As fast as the ranks of the solicitors have grown, the machinery has grown with them. Reviewing the development of these technological wonders will help us understand the extent to which they have revolutionized fund-raising and have made possible the phenomenal volume and variety of today's appeals.

Each of these technological milestones has a history of its own, but the basic steps in these histories are very similar, and include the following:

1. The invention itself, the breakthrough
2. The perfecting of the device, and its subsequent introduction to the market
   - This step usually requires a great deal of up-front investment capital. The risk is significant, but is offset by the promise of rewards (often enhanced by patent protection) that will accrue if the device is widely accepted.

3. Universal acceptance and usage of the device
   - People en masse begin to use the device; the average home has it.
4. Usage of the device by fund-raisers
   - Secular fund-raisers first appropriate the device; Christian fund-raisers then follow their lead.

The primary advances have been those made in radio, television, and movies, in the efficiency of air travel and the telephone, and in computer technology.

Radio
In almost all technological development, the "thinking-it-through" stage requires the most time, and the development of the radio was no exception. Although Michael Faraday's theory about the electromagnetic field was announced in 1832 — and thus suggested the possibility of radio — it wasn't until sixty years later that Oliver Lodge demonstrated the first radio communication system. Shortly after this initial invention — in 1903 — Guglielmo Marconi, popularly credited with developing practical radiowave transmission, successfully sent a message across the Atlantic.

Once the radio was properly developed and introduced to the market, it took little time to catch on. In Pittsburgh in 1920, Frank Conrad inaugurated the first daily-scheduled radio broadcast intended for public entertainment, and this produced a significant demand for receivers. By 1924, when H. V. Kaltenborn was nationally broadcasting election returns, radio had arrived as a significant — even commonplace — communication medium. The Christian community didn't wait long to make use of radio. A station offering entirely religious programming came into existence within a single year of Conrad's first broadcast in Pittsburgh. This station was part of the Church of the Pilgrim in Washington, D.C., the forerunner of the National Presbyterian Church. The first established religious station that is still in continuous operation today is KFUO, which broadcasts from Clayton, Missouri (a suburb of St. Louis). KFUO went on the air in December 1924.

Today there are 1,086 stations listing themselves with the

Federal Communications Commission as stations devoted to religious formats and programs. A very small portion of these are devoted to world religions other than Christianity, and to various cults, but the majority of these stations are Christian and evangelical.

Television

Television was in the theoretical and developmental stages when radio was being publicly introduced and growing in popularity. V. K. Zworykin, a Russian immigrant who came to America in 1917, developed the key components of both the camera (iconoscope) and the receiver (kinescope). He exhibited his electronic television system in 1923, but it was the great improvements he made in 1929 and 1931 that made modern television possible. The first television broadcast meant for public reception took place in New York City in 1941; the major networks formed in the late forties.

Christian appropriation of television, unlike that of radio, took some time, due largely to the heavy costs involved in producing and airing television broadcasts, as well as to the severe limitation in the number of broadcast channels available prior to the advent of UHF and cable facilities. The first Christian station, WCBN in Portsmouth, Virginia, finally appeared in 1959. Today there are thirty-five Christian stations airing expressly religious programming throughout their air time.

• • • •

In describing these stations, we do not mean to ignore all the Christian programming on secular stations. Although the Christian station represents the ultimate single investment in radio or television, secular station use represents a great proportion of all Christian broadcasting, and can mean reaching an audience less exposed to the gospel. Knowledgeable industry sources estimate that between 2800 and 2900 Christian programs (local and network) air weekly on secular radio and TV. Just over half of these are broadcasts from local churches sponsoring their Sunday morning service or a message from their pastor.

Both radio and television broadcasts play a unique part in Christian fund-raising. Of course, each medium has its unique purposes and idiosyncrasies, but radio and television fund-raising stands apart from the others because of what the money is wanted for: with few exceptions, broadcast fund-raisers want the listener or viewer to support a ministry aimed right back at himself. You may receive an appeal letter from a youth ministry, see a film telling the story of a foreign mission's needs, or get a telephone call from an educational institution asking for your help; but the vast majority of *broadcast* fund-raising reaching you asks that you support a broadcast ministry aimed directly at you. Teaching, preaching, counseling, musical performance, testimonies, and interviews — it's all intended for you, the American evangelical.

Unlike foreign missionaries and any other Christian workers beyond the local church, the Christian broadcaster develops an *exchange* relationship with those to whom he appeals for funds. He knows that a large number of the listeners or viewers appreciate a particular program: they feel helped by it and are grateful. As a result, they want to support the program so that they can keep enjoying it — and so that others with similar needs and tastes can enjoy it, too. And they definitely have the money to do so, because they are largely American evangelicals, that group which contributes over half of all funds going to parachurch Christian work all over the world.

For the more successful Christian programs — those attracting and holding large audiences — this exchange relationship has meant significant income over the years. In fact, in more than one case, support monies have continually exceeded all costs by a substantial margin. Certain program producers enjoying such success have felt led by God to channel accumulating funds into support for foreign missions and other work. For example, the Back-to-the-Bible Broadcast, a very popular and well-established program airing daily on more than 500 stations across America, has offered partial financial support to a number of foreign missionaries for over thirty years. This group currently supports about 270 missionaries in this way; it also produces programs in foreign languages for international distribution.

Other broadcast organizations, similarly successful but less exemplary, have simply let the money pile up, sometimes accumulating lavish facilities or equipment, or financing a jump from radio to television. Certainly we can't say categorically that all such money is misspent—only that it perhaps could be *better spent*.

But it is inescapably true that *all* broadcasting requires a great deal of money simply to sustain itself, primarily because of key two factors: production costs and broadcasting costs. Under the careful scrutiny of the Federal Communications Commission, both religious program producers and *some* stations seek listener and viewer support within a structure so complex that it would take volumes to fully explain it. We therefore offer instead a simplified list of the basic descriptive facts of the system:

1. Programs are produced by organizations devoted solely to programming *and* by stations themselves.

2. Religious stations are commercial (financing operations by charging for the time to air the program) *and* non-commercial (financing operations through listener/viewer support).

3. Secular stations are commercial *and* non-commercial.

4. Christian program producers put their programs on all four types of stations.

5. Because someone (usually the program producer) has paid for the time on a commercial station, he may therefore "advertise" directly—i.e., ask listeners for money.

6. In the case of non-commercial stations, only the station itself may solicit support of its operations. The program producer may only motivate listeners to write in, and then solicit funds by some other means from those who respond.

7. Very rarely do non-broadcast ministries use broadcast time to raise funds. The exceptions are these:

a. The larger, more aggressive relief ministries and a few others have used television for telethon-like appeals.

b. Organizations whose broad ministries include broadcast work will showcase all of their work and appeal for funds on commercial radio and TV.

c. Broadcast organizations that also support missions and other similar work will use commercial stations to present these needs.

The Motion Picture

Although the motion picture is functionally unrelated to the several media that depend on electromagnetism (the radio, telegraph, and telephone), it, too, was developed during the last quarter of the nineteenth century. Notable in film history is the year 1889, when Thomas Edison demonstrated his kinetoscope, using a flexible film supplied by Eastman. The Europeans were equally inventive with film, however, and the first commercial projection actually took place in Paris in 1895. The first motion picture telling a story appeared a year later (again in France), but what launched the movie industry in America was the appearance—several years later—of what has become a classic in silent films: *The Great Train Robbery*. The "talkies" appeared in the twenties, and that same decade brought technological refinements that put film within reach of groups with less than Hollywood-size budgets: teachers, documentary makers, industrial groups—and fund-raisers.

The first expressly evangelical Christian film appeared in the later 1930's. Its subject was John Bunyan's *Pilgrim's Progress*, and it was produced by C. O. Baptista, generally regarded as the pioneer in evangelical motion pictures. About ten years later, Bob Pierce, founder of World Vision, traveled to China and brought back the footage that was made into a film entitled *China Challenge*. Pierce showed this film again and again in raising the money that launched the organization that became World Vision. In doing so he established the basic strategy that Christian fund-raisers use today.

In fact, the motion picture is a medium of special value to the fund-raiser because, through a film's distribution, he can exercise a degree of audience selectivity not possible with other mass media. To take full advantage of this factor, the fund-raiser using film makes fewer messages on a grander scale: he spends more on the limited number of messages delivered to his easily targeted audience, and thus can make each message more powerful. By nature the motion picture is *not* an educator: it is not strong on communicating information. What it does best is powerfully communicate mood and emotion. And that is precisely why it is relied upon so often on fund-raising occasions—from the evening service in the local church to large, elaborate dinners—to pave the way for a successful appeal. Usually an offering is taken on the spot, although pledges are also accepted at larger events.

Because of film's potentially powerful combination of audience selectivity and emotional impact, the fund-raiser has revered film from the beginning. But because of its prohibitive cost, film has basically been used only by those larger organizations that could afford it. When professional production of even the simplest film (shot on location) costs a minimum of $2,000.00 per minute, a fund-raiser must have the resources to put that film to essentially continuous use in order to make it more attractive per dollar of cost than some other, less expensive means of fund-raising. An organization large enough to put several copies to continuous use is all the more likely to choose film. But that use must be truly continuous, because a film's effective life is short: clothing styles, models of cars, and dozens of similar marks of western society will date a movie quickly.

Because frequent usage is so important in determining the effectiveness of a fund-raising film, efficient distribution of such a film is essential. General-interest Christian films are distributed by firms that specialize in just that—distributing Christian films for rental use. But these distributors almost never handle Christian *fund-raising* films, because such films aren't rented. Usually, then, the organization that made the film is responsible for distributing it effectively.

How a film gets to a showing is a strategic question, because money is often collected directly after a fund-raising film is shown. If it's sent in the mail, then who is going to collect the offering for the fund-raiser? Of course, this isn't a problem for the groups large enough to have regional fund-raising representatives, but it has been a problem for some smaller groups. In fact, in the past some groups have used local performers to take up the collection—people who could deliver a short but effective plea after the film. These pitchmen were motivated with a promise that they would receive a percentage of the funds collected. In more than one unfortunate instance, the performer received as much as fifty percent of the offering.

Because economies of scale make film a better tool for the

larger fund-raiser, film has not been used for fund-raising as much as other media have. Nevertheless, it is likely that almost everyone reading this book has seen at least one Christian fund-raising film.

Air Travel

Few — if any — technological advances were longer in the "dreaming" and theorizing stage than flying. For many centuries man thought seriously about how he could fly. Finally, in the fifteenth century Leonardo da Vinci began pitting his genius against the problem, and the desire to fly became truly common. But it was not until the eighteenth century that Swiss physicist Daniel Bernoulli discovered the effect — known by his name — that enabled development of the airfoil and thereby the airplane wing.

Despite this strategic discovery, air travel developed much more slowly than many other technological inventions because failure so often resulted in much more than mere frustration: injury and death were frequent. The first flights were unpowered, much like the hang glider flights of today, and so were dangerously dependent on the fits of the wind. The significance of the Wright Brothers' flight thus lies in a combination of two factors: it was a powered flight — and they survived. Feats like this — epitomized by Lindbergh's gloriously successful transatlantic flight — made flight increasingly attractive. And flight's promise of a tremendous saving in travel time also spurred on the aviator and fired the enthusiasm of his would-be passenger.

In 1914, in fact, the first paying passenger climbed aboard an airplane. He flew from St. Petersburg to Tampa and back on the maiden passenger flight of the Tampa-St. Petersburg Air Boat Company. In these early days of air travel there was often more mail aboard — by weight — than passengers. But when the first jet airliner began service in 1958, air travel truly came of age. Jet propulsion, by providing greater speed and greater stability in difficult weather, made air travel safe and attractive to millions.

You may be wondering how air travel can be classified as a fund-raising medium. Be assured that it can be. Remember that Harry Truman was the last political candidate to "whistle-stop" by train; that was in 1948. Today a political candidate crisscrosses the country, arriving at scheduled times coordinated with local events and circumstances in order to maximize crowd size and press coverage. The candidate can literally speak at breakfast in Boston, lunch in Los Angeles, and dinner in Dallas. And so can the charisma-filled leader of a Christian ministry, a leader whose very presence generates a fund-raising event—often even when nothing else will. He may appear at church services, banquets, seminars, retreats, and conferences; but he can also make local radio and television appearances, hold press conferences, and arrange meetings with key donors, because ease of travel makes it possible for him to be amazingly and effectively mobile. Today an individual can even maintain administrative leadership of an organization and still travel to make occasional fund-raising appearances elsewhere. Or, leaving the administrative duties to someone else, he can travel continually, appearing at two or three events each day in chosen population areas.

The Telephone

The average American is more familiar with the development of the telephone than with most other important inventions of that period when communications development exploded. This is true partly because the story of Alexander Graham Bell and Thomas Watson working tirelessly together in a small laboratory has been told and retold by the Bell System public relations machinery—and not inappropriately. What fewer people know is that Thomas Edison, another founder of what is today a huge corporate structure, developed a strategic part of the telephone. In the late 1870's and early 1880's, Bell made possible electromagnetic transmission of speech, while Edison created the amplifier. Following various changes and refinements, the first transcontinental telephone call took place in 1915, but the telephone wasn't economically feasible for popular use until 1918. Figures prove its remarkable popularity since then: by 1960 there were 75 million telephones in the U.S. and 141 million in the world; today, over 400 million telephones are in use worldwide.

The telephone serves a unique function in fund-raising be-

cause it is the only medium by which both the fund-raiser and
the donor commonly initiate the contact—each in different
circumstances. The donor uses the phone, at the fund-raiser's
instigation, as a response device. Frequently he responds to
fund-raising events on television, many of them the work of
Christian organizations. Usually a bank of telephones manned
by volunteers is prominently pictured, and the viewer is urged
to call in immediately with a pledge. When he calls he is asked
to give his name and address so that a reminder can be sent to
him; the volunteer will also add this name to the organization's
mailing list.

In reaching out to his constituency, the fund-raiser uses the
telephone frequently for two purposes. One is to communicate
with a regular donor who gives quite generously. This donor
should get more than a personal letter, yet he doesn't give
enough to make a personal visit from an organizational representative a financially feasible possibility. The fund-raiser also
relies on the telephone when a financial crisis is at hand. He
realizes that in a short time he can use the telephone to reach
numerous supporters who are sympathetic and committed to
the cause. Aware of the effectiveness of this kind of plea, a
number of organizations that rely on a relatively close relationship with a small constituency have fallen into a pattern of
annual crisis and annual phone calls. (Possibly out of embarrassment, some of these groups have given this annual event a
positive name to dispel the notion of recurrent crisis. This is
probably a big mistake. If they can't avoid the annual crisis,
they should probably not take the sackcloth off from it, because
then their constituency tends to lose empathy for their cause.

Of course, the telephone's value to the fund-raiser is not
restricted to the two situations we describe above—as a known
or potential donor, you may receive calls for a variety of reasons. But one factor will almost always apply: you will at least
have heard of the soliciting organization. Even with one-minute
rates and WATS lines, organizations can't afford to pick up the
phone book and begin random calling on behalf of a ministry.

The Computer
While it was easy to imagine oneself flying before the plane

was invented, or talking to a friend miles away even before the telephone existed, it was in many ways impossible for a man to imagine himself programming a non-existent computer. For, as you may have heard it said, electronic data processing never brought us a new way to work — merely a faster one. It gives us the benefit of great speed, ever-accelerating speed, mind-boggling speed — but only speed.

Remarkable as it may seem, a digital computer was proposed already in 1834 by a man named Charles Babbage, but his idea went undeveloped for over one hundred years until other necessary developments took place. Finally, during World War II, the first automatic general-purpose digital computer was built: the Harvard IBM Automatic Sequence-Controlled Calculator. Developed as a wartime aid, it was mechanical rather than electronic. It accomplished multiplication in approximately four seconds and division in about eleven seconds. Calculation times for today's electronic computers are given in nanoseconds — seconds to the minus ninth power — so our assertion of mind-boggling speed is hardly an exaggeration.) The first electronic computer was produced soon after the war, in 1946.

It probably isn't possible to express in layman's terms — or any other terms — the full extent of the computer's effect on twentieth-century commerce of all kinds, including fund-raising. Yet, with the computer about to enter the household, its effect on society may well be only beginning.

If we attempt to give a general description of the computer's functional contribution, we should say first that speed is merely the means, not the end. The "machine," as data processing practitioners lovingly refer to it, stores tremendous amounts of information, executes innumerable calculations with that information, and then stores the new information resulting from the calculations — and it does all this automatically. Its primary benefits are two-fold. First, it enables its "masters" to keep much more information at hand, and therefore to know much more about what they are doing. Second, it eliminates the need for most of the people who manually accomplished the calculating and filing before the computer age. Most organizations see two primary financial benefits of computerization: they need fewer employees (which reduces costs), and thus they have more capital to invest in improving their imformation-gathering system and related computer functions.

As you might guess, the computer's most common functions in fund-raising are the storage, maintenance, and improvement of mailing lists, and the performance of clerical functions necessary to fund-raising. But it has other capabilities that are much more sophisticated and impressive. A good example is the computer's ability to merge two or more mailing lists (often involving a million or more names), find and purge any duplicated names or addresses, and then print out mailing labels for the total of unduplicated names. Often a third list, that of the group's constituency, is involved as a "suppress file." The computer "suppresses" production of a label for any name found on the purchased lists that is already on the constituency list. When the responses from a fund-raising appeal come in, the computer can categorize them by amount given, and then qualify and recategorize, if appropriate, all donor names stored within its memory banks. Lately the computer also writes letters — or at least mass-produces "personalized" letters. The machine can "personalize" a form letter stored in its memory by inserting in it appropriate information about a specific person — information that is "fed" to it or, like the letter, is stored in its memory. Inserted information might include a list of the individual's preferences or his special interests, the characteristics of his town or city, demographic data about him, etc.

The machine isn't foolproof when it performs such tasks, however; its performance is only as good as its information. When its information is wrong, the machine can make some unintentionally humorous mistakes. A prime example is the letter sent by the large fund-raising organization of a well-known television preacher. Sent to a franchisee of a national fried chicken operation, it addressed the recipient several times as "Chicken," coming up with memorable lines like "It is dedication like yours, Chicken. . . ." And several years ago the computer also malfunctioned occasionally because it could work internally (doing the calculations electronically) much faster than it could absorb the data — and far faster than it could print out the processed data. But new high-speed printing developments have largely corrected this problem; in computer letter production, these advances make the machine able to produce more letters faster than ever. In this area particularly, the Christian fund-raiser is adopting such advances with speed and determination.

In fact, the Christian fund-raiser is in many ways adopting the techniques of his secular counterpart. As evidence of this fact we offer the following list of seminars and workshops within seminars, a list drawn from the countless promotional pieces that we have collected over a period of several years. This is only a partial listing that covers only the highlights of the brochures:

Topics of workshops
- Researching the prospective contributor
- The value of an inquiry name
- The role of the fund-raising consulting firm vs. your development department
- How to gain additional income from. . . .
- Increasing the growth of a large-donor list
- What you can learn from commercial mailers
- How we built our list and evaluated our results
- Setting up and maintaining a deferred-giving program
- Tax techniques for deferred giving
- Successfully soliciting funds from foundations
- The impact of proposed AICPA accounting rules on religious organizations
- The effect of the 1976 Tax Reform Act on a planned-giving program
- Communications problems between fund-raisers and computer programmers
- Communicating fund-raising ideas to the computer programmer

Topics of seminars
- Basic computer techniques for fund-raisers
- Computer letter mechanics
  1. Elements of a computer letter
     — window vs. closed-face envelope
     — brochure enclosure vs. no enclosure
     — one-page vs. a multi-page letter
     — stamp vs. meter postage
     — first-class vs. non-profit postage

    2. Types of fonts available
    3. Converting to upper and lower case (a computer normally prints all upper case)
    4. How to personalize the letter
    5. How to program the computer for punctuation, abbreviation, etc.
    6. How to make the letter look typewritten
    7. New laser-beam and ink-jet spray techniques
- The importance of copy in computer letters
    1. When to use the person's name
    2. How to thank the donor for his last contribution
    3. Two letters for the price of one: the use of carbon-copy letters
    4. How to insert demographics and personal notes into the copy
- "Cleaning" your donor lists
- How to develop and organize a special fund-raising event
- Where do you go when you've used all of the lists?
- What additional fund-raising programs you should implement (a discussion of the entire range of solicitation techniques)
- Goal-setting: the basis for responsible accountability
- Response devices
- Guidelines and ethics for religious fund-raisers

Printing and Mailing Equipment

These technological wonders go unheralded and seem unspectacular because their sophistication has occurred gradually, not in major breakthroughs. For this reason, almost no one knows how this machinery developed, and only those in the business themselves know about its amazing capabilities: that it can perform ink-jet printing and laser-beam color separations you've never read about in your magazines or seen on television. It is a technology that gets little or no publicity — yet it is the technology most responsible for the kind of fund-raising appeal we get most often: the appeal letter.

We usually appreciate getting letters from those organizations we know and heartily support. Such letters are often hand-typed, hand-signed, and in all respects are like a letter from a friend. But, instead, we usually get those letters that have been processed and sent out en masse — those that come from groups who have purchased our name and address and have then sent us an appeal for a ministry with which we are largely unfamiliar. Because we and most of the thousands upon thousands of others receiving such a letter have little or no previous knowledge of the sender, we are, mathematically speaking, relatively unlikely to respond. And the fund-raiser sending the letter is well aware of this fact. Consequently, he realizes that the gifts received from the few who do respond must more than pay for producing and sending letters to all the others who do not respond. For this reason each letter must be *very* inexpensive to produce and mail. It is within these restrictive circumstances that modern mailing technology makes its most profound contribution to fund-raising.

Because the U.S. Post Office decides what it will cost to get a letter to the recipient, the only financial variable that the fund-raiser has to work with is the cost of producing the letter — addressing it, stamping it, and getting it ready to go. This is precisely the function of modern mailing equipment, which has developed these capabilities:

- Folds letters at speeds up to seven per second
- Gathers material and stuffs it into envelopes at up to two units per second
- Applies address labels to envelopes as fast as seven per second
- Seals the envelope and applies postage at up to three envelopes per second

Although there are countless other examples, what best illustrates this amazing speed is the situation in which disaster strikes and time is of the essence — when, for example, a hurricane strikes Honduras or an earthquake hits Italy or Japan. Because donors naturally respond in relation to the time elapsed before they receive the appeal for relief money, groups doing relief work are organized to take advantage of every second — and legitimately so. Given production minimums of two letters per second, the sophisticated mailing house can put out over 100,000 letters — per production line — in a sixteen-hour period. If the fund-raiser is willing to pay the premium for emergency service, he can easily mail a million pieces within 24 hours of the time that he has the letter produced.

There you have, then, a quick overview of the media that deliver most of the fund-raising messages that we receive each day—a look at the origins and modern-day usefulness of each. Now, finally, let's look at them in a manner that relates them to each other.

Like any promotional message, a fund-raising appeal must be limited in cost by the level of financial response anticipated from the particular audience involved. In projecting total response, the fund-raiser must project both the percentage of the audience that will respond and the size of the average gift. In most cases he will know the size of the audience, but in some cases he will have to estimate it. He must then limit, accordingly, his message cost per audience member. A more expensive message can influence the size of the average gift, but the quality of the audience is a much more decisive factor affecting donation size.

Most promotional messages usually fall between the extremes of the most expensive and least expensive message. The former is aimed at a highly interested and responsive audience, the latter at a mass audience often largely unfamiliar with the communicating organization. In the language of mass communications, the former is termed a "rifle" approach; the latter is called the "shotgun" approach. The rifle approach aims at specific, carefully selected individuals, and each message is specially composed and crafted with care; the shotgun approach involves sending a mass-produced message to a mass audience. Below is a "rifle/shotgun" continuum that illustrates some of the more common tactics of fund-raisers. Each message unit mentioned is cheaper than the previous one.

FROM RIFLE TO . . .

1. The head of the organization flies to another part of the country to court an important potential donor or foundation.

2. The deferred-giving department of an organization offers a free seminar on wills, trusts, and annuities to anyone interested in attending it. Seminar participants who indicate an interest in naming the fund-raising organization in such commitments are given free help in implementing them.

3. A local member of the fund-raiser's field staff makes a personal visit to a long-time faithful supporter to solicit another gift.

4. The most "visible" person in the organization is brought to a city for an event. Dinner is served and a fund-raising film is shown; an offering is taken and pledges are received. (This event is much less expensive if the guests pay for their own food.)

5. Someone in the organization with the ability and experience to do so composes a lengthy personal letter to a single individual, a letter replete with personal chitchat and reminiscences as well as the appeal.

6. A telephone call is made to a faithful supporter asking for help, possibly stressing a special need.

7. A series of letters is individually typed by a typewriter with a memory. Each letter is hand-signed and sent first-class with stamp postage.

8. The computer puts out a sizable volume of "personalized" letters, mechanically signed with a signature device.

9. A completely machine-printed letter is sent non-profit bulk rate to 100,000 people whose names have come from a purchased list.

10. An advertisement soliciting funds is placed in an evangelical magazine.

11. A fund-raising telethon is aired over a secular commercial station. A Christian commercial station would have higher audience potential per viewer for the fund-raiser, but his message cost per viewer would be proportionately higher, too, because in most cases the audience would be smaller.

. . . SHOTGUN

• CHAPTER FOUR •

THE PRINCIPAL ABUSES OF CHRISTIAN FUND-RAISING

The primary difference between the wise steward and other donors is his realization—sometimes subconscious—that the most effective ministry is often *not* the best fund-raiser. He recognizes that there is not necessarily a correlation between the ability to minister and the ability to raise money to minister. And the significance of this truth becomes all the greater when we realize that the entire arsenal of fund-raising skills has become available to any organization, of any quality, that lacks money and wants to grow.

In the preceding chapters we have explained the history of fund-raising and the tools of the modern fund-raiser; in this chapter and the next we want to establish a base of common information that we can draw on in later chapters. First of all, we should talk about *abuses* of the fund-raising mechanism. More than any other factors, these abuses blur distinctions between organizations and encourage well-meaning Christian stewards to let substantial portions of their limited financial resources fall into the wrong hands.

The fund-raising mechanism is abused in two basic ways:

1. By the organizations that succumb to the pressures of the fund-raising struggle—a struggle intensified by the continuing proliferation of groups competing for the available money.

2. By the numerous financially successful organizations that fail to deliver on their promises to minister because of fraudulent motives, inability (especially administrative incompetence), or doctrinal misrepresentation.

To put it another way, many abuses of the fund-raising mechanism (and of the donor) are inadvertent—and many are not.

Those abuses provoked by the pressures of the struggle are the errors and bad habits that both fund-raiser and steward fall prey to when they negotiate with each other. Both sides often then compound the other's errors by complying with them. Let's examine two examples. One common abuse perpetrated by the fund-raiser depends for its success on a common bad habit of the steward. It is the practice we call "hot button" fund-raising, which stems from a pervasive problem: too many donors don't determine in advance which groups they are going to support, but simply wait to be influenced by poignant brochures and letters. As a result, they simply react emotionally to the appeals they receive, giving when the emotional jolt exceeds a certain level. Five or six types of ministry have particular potential for maximizing this emotional impact; shrewd fund-raiser emphasis of these ministries is thus called "hot button" fund-raising.

Predictably, the ministry most frequently highlighted because of its emotional appeal is the care of orphaned and destitute children. Few human beings can resist the plaintive face of a helpless child, one so undeserving of what has befallen him. This appeal is so powerful that an entire industry sprang up to plead the cause of children orphaned by the Korean War. Several years ago the U.S. government decided to investigate this phenomenon when certain abuses became apparent — such as certain groups describing children as "orphans" when they actually had one or both parents living. Not all organizations were guilty of such misrepresentation, of course, but the problem did seem to be getting out of hand. For this reason the Korean government itself staged a crackdown, closing a number of American-operated institutions it knew were disreputable, and working hard to shed its image as the impoverished "orphan capital." Factors of need also intervened, and major organizations began to concentrate their efforts on more pressing problems in such places as Southeast Asia, Africa, and Bangladesh. The reason for this example is not denunciation but illustration of our point: with the appeal of the destitute child strong enough to spawn an industry, it is not hard to see how an organization with a hand in this work could succumb to the temptation to strongly emphasize this ministry in its fund-raising appeals and neglect to inform donors about efforts equally important but less emotionally persuasive.

Other efforts with "hot button" appeal include the following:

- Confrontational evangelism — gospel presentation through large meetings attended by huge crowds.
- Distribution of religious literature, with emphasis on quantity.
- Construction of new buildings — especially hospitals or organizational headquarters — in countries or regions of spiritual/physical need. The buildings apparently offer the promise of creating a Christian "presence" in the area.

Obviously, these "hot button" appeals each emphasize an important element in God's work on earth, and cannot be neglected simply because fund-raisers play upon them. For you, a steward responsible to God for your giving, the only solution is to see that they don't play upon *you* with these highly emotional appeals. You must thoughtfully examine the *makers* of the appeals to make sure that they are in fact filling the need that they emphasize.

But if fund-raisers are sometimes guilty of pushing these "hot buttons" too often, donors are equally guilty of "mis-giving." A particularly bad financial habit is that of *monthly giving*. Apparently, the idea behind monthly giving is to demonstrate faithful support — yet it is these bit-by-bit installments that raise processing costs and waste money. Despite its drawbacks, this habit is astonishingly pervasive: to many donors it is an unquestioned standard practice. It has never occurred to hundreds of thousands of conscientious stewards that there is a better way to give their money.

Unfortunately, the fund-raiser has strongly reinforced this habit. In fact, most forthright and capable people with years of experience in evangelical fund-raising — though they would probably agree with many other points we make — would not support our opposition to monthly giving. Take Moody Bible Institute, for example. Certainly no more honest and careful a Christian organization is raising funds today. For almost 100 years, Moody has been a model of consistent wisdom and discretion, and we use Moody as an example here only to indicate the pervasiveness of the stress on monthly giving. Currently Moody uses the theme "Monthly for Moody," asking donors to request a set of twelve envelopes to ensure their monthly donations.

What is wrong with monthly giving? Precisely this: it obliges the recipient organization to make twelve "trips to the bank" instead of one to four (the trips made for yearly or tri-monthly donations). As pointed out earlier, the average cost of processing a gift[1] — of *any* size — is the same: between ninety-five cents and a dollar. Therefore, if you send your favorite ministry $5.00 per month, you are contributing only $4.00 per month to the work itself, or $48.00 per year. If you would send that annual total of $60.00 in one lump sum, you would be contributing $59.00 toward the actual ministry. If you sent your gift in two installments, the effective total would be $58.00.

But the fact is that numerous organizations besides Moody encourage the monthly giving that costs them significant percentages of their intake, proof that fund-raisers believe the monthly giving habit is virtually unchangeable. Defenders of monthly giving often say, "But they need the money every month!" But we doubt that many ministries would choose to forfeit twenty percent of an annual gift to processing costs — not if they really thought they had a choice.

What strengthens and encourages these errors and bad habits is the relationship between the evangelical donor and the fund-raiser, which is marred by an imbalance in trust and respect. The fund-raiser trusts the donor — as one trusts a lamb — but he lacks respect for him. This lack of respect is not unfounded: reacting emotionally, largely without information, the average donor has never earned his respect. The donor, on the other hand, too often shows more trust in and respect for the fund-raiser than the latter has ever earned. This blind faith is probably the result of excessive Christian charity: many evan-

---

[1]Processing includes the steps of opening, recording, accounting, receipting, and depositing the gift. Some organizations seek to combat the costs of monthly giving by receipting the gifts of a monthly giver only once a year. This practice reduces processing costs by approximately twenty percent.

gelicals try to assume the best about *anything* calling itself Christian, orthodox, or evangelical. As donors, these people seemingly choose to ignore any hints of fund-raising abuse, to hear and see no evil. As a result, fund-raisers who might otherwise behave in a thoroughly upright manner (especially those representing truly worthy organizations) observe this continuing failure of the donor to exercise care in giving and so yield to the pressure of competition, allowing themselves to compete "blow for blow" with the other, less reputable fund-raisers.

Sensing this capacity for blind trust in their donors, the majority of today's fund-raisers make, and act upon, two assumptions that show a great lack of respect for the donor:

1. The appeal *must* be emotional — emotion must be central to whatever is said. *Facts*, even the good news of success in ministry, should get secondary emphasis.

2. The donor would be alarmed to learn how much money a given organization is raising (annually) and so should not find out about these totals.

This latter conclusion apparently arises from the fund-raiser's belief that the donor favors equal distribution — that he thinks that the money should be divided more or less evenly among competing groups so that everybody gets his fair share. We disagree with this assumption. It is probably true that donors would be alarmed to learn about *idle* money, especially in the coffers of groups proclaiming dire needs; but if the recipient organization uses all gifts to further its work, we do not believe the average donor is alarmed by the size or total amount of receipts. Rather, he views the organization's "wealth" as a sign of encouraging success in the Lord's work.

Many of the above errors are basically inadvertent, but other bad practices plaguing fund-raising are purposeful. In fact, of at least equal consequence to the "errors and bad habits" of donor and fund-raiser are the carefully planned manipulations of the donor by the fund-raiser. Earlier we listed three ways in which the donor is often shortchanged. These weaknesses and deceptions are strongly related to the four basic kinds of charities that are described by Helen O'Rourke, the head of the charitable agencies branch of the Better Business Bureau. Ms.

O'Rourke believes that almost every charity can be defined in one of the following ways:

1. well-intentioned, well-managed
2. well-intentioned, poorly managed
3. operated with little charitable intent, poorly managed
4. clearly fraudulent

It is Ms. O'Rourke's contention, as it is ours, that the operations bent on total fraud — on pulling off a "scam" — are few in number. The biggest proportion of cases brought to the attention of the BBB monitoring service fall into category three — those having little charitable intent.[2] Below we discuss the three most prominent kinds of flawed organizations that the typical donor will encounter.

FRAUDULENT ORGANIZATIONS

Webster's Dictionary defines *fraud* as "the means by which deceit is practiced," and as a "false presentation which deceives and is intended to deceive." It has been established beyond doubt that fraud has been and still is perpetrated by purportedly evangelical organizations. But just what does go on? What is false about the presentations made? Specifically, is it ever total misrepresentation — a case of "take the money and run," in which the organization uses none of the money to minister? In fact, this is hardly ever the case.

The "why not" is obvious if you think for a minute about the consequences of obvious fraud. When a confidence man pulls off a big "sting," he has to get out before the deceived catch on. Fraudulent "Christian" operators are not about to put themselves in the position of having to run for it. They usually follow a shrewd, highly sophisticated plan: they siphon off a sizable portion of their receipts, maintain high "costs," invest a small portion of the money in legitimate Christian work, reveal as little as possible about their financial situation — and continue to rake in the profits.

Some of the worst groups are willing to make thoroughly

[2]From the *FRM Weekly*, January 4, 1978, p. 2.

false claims, but for the most part it is a fraud of degree. They are doing what they say they're doing (or, more likely, giving some of the money to a thoroughly legitimate organization that is doing it), but they are not doing this work nearly as widely or thoroughly as they would lead their donor to believe. And therein lies the fraud. The donor is led to believe that *most* of his money is going to Christian work, that he is supporting much more activity than actually exists. Usually the most common vehicles of this misrepresentation are fund-raising magazines aimed at an organization's constituency — and free of charge, of course. Because almost all parachurch organizations publish a promotional periodical of some sort, it is not hard for the black sheep to hide among the flock. *Eternity* magazine, aware of the scores of such publications received by its readers, used its February 1979 issue to explain how to find relief from "the missionary magazines."

But it is extremely important not to lump all such publications together, because many are of the highest character. *Decision*, from the Billy Graham Association; *In Other Words*, from the Wycliffe Translators; and *The Evangelist*, from Latin America Mission — all of these are very informative, and win frequent awards from the Evangelical Press Association. And, fortunately, these are just a few of the many reputable magazines currently published. Membership in the EPA is a strong indication of the legitimate intentions of such publications.

But existing side by side with these publications are magazines that misrepresent ministries. Very likely destined for just such a magazine are the pictures mentioned in Chapter 1: the shots of public buildings in a foreign capital destined to be misrepresented as orphanages. The layout of such pictures frequently follows a pattern: it shows huge crowds, apparently attending a mass meeting, but rarely includes an article or caption informing the reader of the time and place of that rally. The astute reader will wonder if this is mere carelessness — or if the pictures are outdated or represent rallies never held.

An interesting item in our files provides a particularly notable example of potentially paving the way for fraudulent receipt of funds. We happened to get hold of the constitution of one organization, and discovered this remarkable article in it:

> Only donations actually received by or at the international office shall be considered as organizational assets or income. Any and all funds, properties, etc., donated specifically to or received by any individual members or officers shall be construed as their personal income unless transferred into the organization's control for general, or specific, use in ministries of the organization.

We cannot conclude that this clause was necessarily developed to cover abuse, but it certainly could work that way. Nor can we say that such a clause is always misused, but it seems safe to say that whatever the reasons for its inclusion in this constitution, the benefit to both the donor and the ministry is certainly unclear. What the jargon of the phrase means is that a duly authorized representative of this organization can "legally" keep every cent of what he personally secures in contributions to its activities. And a possible result of such a provision is this: if a member of the inner circle isn't satisfied with his present income, he can hit the speaking circuit, hold a few meetings on behalf of the organization — and pocket the proceeds.

As we have said, very little blatantly fraudulent use of donations occurs — but when someone from a group like this shows up in your evening church service and takes an offering, remember that the money might not go to the worthy causes he describes; he might just name himself the charity to be supported. Admittedly, this is an extreme example of audacity, of preparing the way for fraud. And it involves a group that, though determined, is relatively small. But their brochures are fairly well written, so they often don't sound significantly different from the materials of hundreds of other groups. If you only knew about them what you read in their carefully worded promotional pieces, you would definitely like them. Remember, too, another unfortunate fact: that this tactic, though audacious, is probably not the worst of its kind.

But for the careful steward, the key question about such examples is not whether they show deception in toto or in degree. Rather, the better question is this: how much of each dollar contributed to *this* organization will support effective Christian work? We advise the steward to look for unfavorable relationships between income and cost—rather than for fraud—for two reasons:

1. Such unfavorable relationships are almost always easier to document than is fraud.

2. Financial inquiries are always a source of much discomfort to the fradulent operator. Each time he must decide whether or not to answer a financial inquiry, he is put a bit more on the defensive and made a little less aggressive—because his numbers, if accurate, are not going to do him much good.

POORLY MANAGED ORGANIZATIONS

Here we are not talking about fund-raising inability, but inability to minister and *ad*minister. These are the organizations that, in Helen O'Rourke's words, are "well-intentioned, poorly managed." In every way, this abuse is the opposite of fraud. This operator's error is anything but intentional, and the organization's goals are only the best—yet the same criticism leveled against fraudulent operations applies here: money is lost.

Unfortunately, news of inability is even scarcer in the evangelical world than news of fraud. The authors of this book have for years been privy to information—heard over the lunch table or in the next office—that makes detection of inability relatively easy. But we are quick to realize that most of our readers spend their working day in different enterprises and aren't going to hear about the latest evangelical embarrassments that are the surest sign of inability. When a large parachurch organization—beloved of its donors, beloved of its board of directors—suddenly cashiers fifty of its personnel on a Friday afternoon, that's an embarrassment. When another group unwillingly stops presumably successful work in another part of the world, that's embarrassment. And that's a clue that the organization is poorly managed. But where does an evangelical layman and steward get such clues? This is not an easy question to answer, but we do deal with it in Chapter 6, in which we explain how to get necessary information about evangelical organizations.

The inability we are looking for is much like the inability that can plague a business run for profit. That business must be able to deliver on the produce or service that it offers. And it needs good administrators who can take in money, keep track of it, pay it out for value received in goods and services, maintain assets, and supervise numerous fellow workers. Significant inability to handle these functions usually means the end of the business. And here is the strategic difference between profit and non-profit businesses: whereas a for-profit business can be destroyed by managerial inability, a non-profit business can blunder on *if* it has adequate fund-raising capabilities. The result: subtle, continuing waste. For this reason, the responsible donor must be especially careful. He can't assume that the mere *existence* of a fund-raising organization vouches for its effectiveness.

Finally, two closing observations on inability may be valuable:

1. Some parachurch groups do have somewhat incompetent administrators, and so their service as ministries is flawed, but, all things considered, poor management is not the threat to your donor dollar that fraud is — or that *doctrinal misrepresentation* is.

2. The fear of owning up to failures in evangelical pursuits is abating somewhat, and determined Christian journalists are carrying forward the banner of the public's right to know. We hope the day is not far off when the evangelical donor gets information about evangelical organizations that is as straightforward as the information he gets about companies whose stock he buys — information that honestly and openly reveals inability and failure.

ORGANIZATIONS GUILTY OF
DOCTRINAL MISREPRESENTATION

Ever since one of us referred to a certain retreat ministry as "Split Hair Ranch" and got a look of dire discomfort from one of that group's staff, we've become increasingly concerned about

the need for evangelicals to understand and appreciate the varying doctrinal views among themselves. But we're not talking
about this matter here. We refer instead to a fund-raiser's full
awareness that his work does not share or support some of the
beliefs important to his targeted donor. We don't need to spend
hours wondering if such abuse is inadvertent or purposeful.
Doctrinal misrepresentation, as we use the term, falls strongly
on the intentional side of the fence. When fund-raisers per-
petrating this kind of dishonesty prepare their appeals for the
evangelical donor, they are thinking "camouflage." Their strategy is to get as close to the donor as possible without attracting
unnecessary attention, making their organizations look much
like the others; then they emphasize underprivileged children,
caring for the poor, and other sorts of work that de-emphasize
doctrinal concerns in the donor's mind. And with those donors
who give only with the heart, such organizations are successful
year after year.

What organizations are among those that have been criti-
cized for using this kind of tactic? They include certain Catholic
groups, such as the Pallottine Fathers of Baltimore; Father Flan-
agan's Boys' Town in Nebraska, long under investigation by the
Omaha World Herald; and the Missionhurst Fathers of Arling-
ton, Virginia. (The Pallottines' notoriety has increased greatly
since their fund-raising leader, Reverend Guido John Corcich,
was indicted for fraud and pleaded guilty.[3]) These organizations
use a clever tactic: they send a discernibly Roman Catholic
mailing to their Catholic donors, but a sort of Christian/non-
sectarian mailing to names on all other lists they can obtain.[4]

Groups like these will frequently use a mailing that contains
one or more "free" gifts: address labels, a calendar, a booklet of
"sunshine verse," possibly some lottery tickets for a drawing for
a car or other expensive gift. The psychology here is obvious:
the fund-raiser figures that such a mailing will make many people feel obligated to send a few dollars just to pay for the

---

[3]The *Baltimore Sun* investigated this group's practices.

[4]For more information, see Gaylord Briley's article, "Catholic Charities
and Protestant Donors," in *Christian Heritage* magazine.

favors — even if they aren't particularly sure about the organization's religious affiliation.

Much more devious fund-raisers are the pert and beaming pawns of the latest cult, who confront anyone and everyone in airports, bus terminals, and other public places from one end of our country to the other.

Especially visible are the "Moonies" of Korean Sun Myung Moon's Unification Church, and the newly westernized Hare Krishna followers. These "youth cults" use high-pressure sales tactics, and will often tell potential donors that money given will support "Christian work among young people," using this and other phrases to disarm people familiar with orthodox Christianity.[5] Most of the people joining these cults are under twenty-five, largely because the Unification faith is a "dormitory religion." The church wants its initiates to be involved in the group's activities every waking moment, and only uncommitted young people have the time for this kind of devotion. And to the many upper-class American youth whose parents largely absented themselves from child-rearing responsibilities — but provided the money for premature mobility — joining these cults can be like finding a family.

We offer this comment on the appeal of youth cults because so many middle-aged adults insist they cannot understand how any young person of normal intelligence can be hooked by these groups. But think of those very adults who join Herbert Armstrong's Church of God — aren't they equally gullible? If the Moonies are judged gullible because they go obediently to the airport day after day to sell flowers or books, what about the Church of God adherents who passively accept the repeated demands for tithe after tithe from their family's income?[6] "But," you say, "the Moonies try for everyone's money without caring whether donors join them or not. Armstrong's group doesn't." But does it really work that way?

[5]See the article in the *New York Times Magazine*, May 30, 1976, p. 24.
[6]Perhaps the past tense would be more accurate here. At the time of this writing, Armstrong's Church of God was in receivership in the California courts, Armstrong had excommunicated his son, Garner Ted, and Armstrong and longtime right-hand man Stanley Radar faced charges of personal use of millions of the church's funds.

True, we wouldn't say that Armstrong's church specifically misrepresents itself, and it is very particular about its members. But in seeking out these members it also appeals to believers beyond that carefully selected number — and receives significant financial support from them.

Have you ever heard of a magazine called *The Plain Truth*? It has functioned for years as a powerful contact tool of Armstrongism — the "leading edge of the funnel," as one observer put it. With many of the faithful tithing, double tithing, and even *triple* tithing, the organization has become rich, and has used some of its money to print literally millions upon millions of copies of this fund-raising tool. And it still has had enough money to pay for Garner Ted Armstrong's frequent television appearances, during which he discusses world events as signs of the impending apocalypse.[7] Both the magazine and the program are directed at readers and viewers *beyond* the circle of Armstrong devotees. Both offer something to the reader/viewer (usually literature explaining "the final days"), and every respondent gets his name on their mailing lists.

Don't allow yourself to believe that these appeals haven't netted contributions from sincere Christian believers — they definitely have. The apocalyptic sound of the Armstrong gospel has strong appeal for many evangelicals burning with the "prophecy fever" so common in the ranks of conservative Christianity — an appeal that the promoters of Armstrongism use to their financial advantage. The Church of God — like numerous other groups of all stripes hunting for money — singles us out for another reason, too: because we evangelical Christians are commonly known to be committed givers, the hunting is considered best in our ranks.

A variation on the theme of doctrinal misrepresentation has developed recently: lack of doctrine, rather than misrepresentation, is the shortcoming of a growing number of fund-raisers who feature a promise that is even stronger than prophecy fever. It is the "give and grow rich" story: God wants you — yes, you! — to be *well-to-do*. Despite our Lord Jesus' repeated upholding of the poor *as* the poor and His repeated warnings

---

[7]We should point out that this program is no longer on the air.

of the dangers of riches, many well-meaning Christians are sufficiently inclined to *want* to believe the "give and grow rich" line that they *do* believe it, and thus develop a donor relationship with one of the groups who propagate it.

This, then, is a summary of fund-raising gone awry. Sometimes inadvertently, sometimes intentionally, the Christian fund-raising procedure is abused—by both fund-raiser *and* donor. Having examined this problem carefully, we should now determine what steps we can take as stewards to assure that these abuses affect our personal stewardship as little as possible.

For the benefit of all, but especially for those not accustomed to frank, open talk about fraud and other abuses in suposedly Christian work, we close this chapter by offering a bibliography of articles written by people who have attempted before us to decry some of these same abuses:

"Caution: Evangelical Swindlers at Work," written by Dr. Clyde W. Taylor in *United Evangelical ACTION*. Article available from the National Association of Evangelicals.

Giving —from the Heart, with the Head, a pamphlet published in August 1973 and available from the Mennonite Board of Missions.

"Korean Orphan Appeal: How Long?" written by Bill Bray in *Christianity Today*, July 28, 1972.

"The Missing Names and the Missions," *Christianity Today*, September 23, 1977, p. 51.

"The Scandal of Evangelical Giving," written by Billy A. Melvin in *United Evangelical ACTION*, Winter 1976.

Articles have also been written about organizations that are not specifically evangelical but that evangelicals are nevertheless drawn to support:

"Charities: Which Ones are Worth Giving to?" *Reader's Digest*, February 1974.

"Probing the Pallottines," *Church & State*, February 1976, p. 17.

Jack Anderson's column of October 3, 1974, in the *Fort Wayne Journal Gazette*.

But perhaps the articles with the most discouraging subject are those that examine the reason why many evangelicals think covering up abuses is "the Christian thing to do":

"Non-Prophet Christian Journalism," written by C. Stephen Board in *Eternity*, February 1977.

"Telling the Truth in Love . . . ," written by Wally Kroeker in *The Christian Leader*, February 15, 1977, p. 2.

Nonetheless, some interesting developments suggest that evangelicals may get better at policing themselves:

"Monthly Memo" in *World Vision*, December 1978, p. 9.

• CHAPTER FIVE •

ESTABLISHING A SOLID FOUNDATION
FOR GIVING

Having reviewed, in the previous chapters, the historical roots and modern technology of the church's fund-raising mechanism and the abuses of this mechanism, we are now ready to spend the remainder of the book carefully delineating the steps a steward can take to build a more effective program of giving.

The old saying "Well begun is half done" is a bit of an overstatement, at least when applied to personal stewardship — but a good beginning is certainly important. We make that "good beginning" by building a solid foundation under the program. And the first and most important stone — the cornerstone — of that solid foundation is our personal certainty that we are giving for truly biblical reasons.

Believers are to give out of heartfelt thanks, obedience, and concern; II Corinthians 8:7-15 is an especially helpful passage in making this point clearly and meaningfully. When we cease to give this way and begin to do so out of some sort of legalistic compulsion to perform as Christians, we are well on the way toward frustration and defeat in our stewardship. Before long this attitude can lead to carelessness in giving, then reduction in giving and, finally, defeat in other areas of our spiritual lives. As we mentioned in our introduction, many traditional stewardship books handle this subject effectively, and for that reason we take the matter no further. But we do include at the end of this chapter a short bibliography of particularly worthwhile treatments of traditional stewardship.

The second stone in a solid foundation is a carefully spelled-out procedure for accumulating and dispersing your stewardship money. If this strikes you as a detail — mere busywork — be assured that it is not. As we explain below, how well you handle accumulation and dispersal of your gifts can significantly affect the success of your stewardship program.

Accumulation

Every steward must begin by deciding what portion of his income he will return to God. To the extent that this giving strains his financial equilibrium (and it should), he will tend to find it difficult to maintain a positive and aggressive attitude toward his stewardship responsibilities. Certainly he must draw on the resources of his personal relationship with God to offset the wear and tear on positive attitude that "giving until it hurts" may bring. But he must recognize another resource, too: while the proper attitude is most influenced by prayer and his walk with God, the manner in which he accumulates the money can also affect his attitude. As you probably know from your own experience, once you are behind in giving it's harder to catch up than it was to stay paid up. And once you're really behind, meeting your goals becomes close to impossible — unless the proportion you are giving is not a financial challenge to you.

What, then, can be done to make accumulation a pillar of your program rather than a pitfall, a joy and not a burden? First, eliminate the two most common and harmful mistakes Christians make in setting money aside for giving:

1. *Don't give out of what is left.*

Historical evidence tells us that the predominant principle guiding stewardship in the first- and second-century church was that of firstfruits.

The key element of firstfruits giving, especially relevant here, is that the first money set aside from periodic income is that going to the Lord's work. The idea is to be certain to "live on the rest" after the Lord's portion is given, rather than planning on giving to God from whatever is left after you have maintained yourself. The latter approach is the way many Christians manage accumulation — and the way they make the first mistake in giving.

This firstfruits approach to accumulation is also an effective means of maintaining a positive attitude toward stewardship. If you "live on the rest," you cannot help but tailor your lifestyle and "needs" to available dollars and not allow yourself to consume what you originally intended for God.

2. Don't tie accumulation to dispersal.

Many people believe they should set aside (accumulate) and give (disperse) their stewardship money the way a baseball player who is in the middle of a double play is supposed to catch and then throw the ball—all in one motion. This is the second big mistake many stewards make.

I do *not* have to give away today what I set aside today. Many people have been pressed into the "gift-money-burns-a-hole-in-your-pocket" school of thought by an overzealous reading of Paul's admonition in II Corinthians 8:11—his urging to "complete" or "finish" the work of providing for the saints at Jerusalem. Such zealots often translate this admonition as "Do it immediately." But in our modern era any group deserving your support is going to be sufficiently well managed to be operating on the basis of an annual budget. In this light, "immediately" becomes any time within the operating year. Those who are concerned that monies be distributed as soon as they are received increase their vulnerability to three specific stewardship problems:

1. *dilution of effect*, due to breaking up a large gift into smaller monthly (or other) units. (We discussed this matter in the previous chapter.)

2. *determining the size of gift by "circumstance"*: If, to avoid dilution of effect, you decide that your total gift to one organization will be everything set aside in one period, then the size of that gift is determined by "circumstance" (i.e., the amount available from that period) and not by careful, prayerful decision on your part.

3. *"getting rid of it"*: This is more aptly described as an error than a problem, and is the worst of the three. It occurs when a steward has money on hand and believes it should go out immediately, but doesn't have any specific recipient in

mind. Eighteen hundred years ago, the *Didache*, a significant second-century Christian document, wisely advised believers to "Let thine alms sweat in thy hand until thou knowest to whom thou givest" — and that advice is equally good today. Fortunately, it's easy to avoid premature giving: simply eliminate simultaneous accumulation and dispersal.

But we do not want to make this matter appear simpler than it is. Accumulation and dispersal are best separated, but they must also be coordinated. (We discuss this coordination below when we talk about dispersal.)

If at this point we were to describe an ideal accumulation procedure, we would mislead more readers than we would help, because stewards (like other people) receive their income in a variety of patterns. Some receive a fixed amount at a fixed interval — weekly, bi-weekly, or monthly. Others receive varying amounts at regular intervals. Still others receive varying amounts at sporadic intervals. The steward must suit his accumulation procedure to his earning pattern.

Nevertheless, one particular technique is sure to help anyone, and it is this: Set stewardship monies aside from income at the time you put that income into the bank (before it gets mixed with the rest of your money). And to accomplish this in the simplest and most helpful manner, set up a separate checking account — an account for stewardship money *only*. Although the convenience of the separate account is significant, the predominant value of it is psychological. Most people will find that because this money is physically separated from the rest of their earnings, it is *gone* — they no longer think of using it for their personal needs and wants.

This tactic has significant potential for helping to make stewardship a positive experience. One of us (Youngren) finds that the separate account allows a freedom akin to "giving somebody else's money away," without short-circuiting any of the joy of sharing. We highly recommend it. If you decide not to establish a separate account, at least keep some continuing written record of how much stewardship money is accumulating in your regular bank account. Although this technical separation of funds will probably not be as meaningful a move to you, it will at least help accomplish the goal of taking the Lord's portion "off the top."

To those who wonder why we make such an issue of setting aside firstfruits in a disciplinary manner, we offer the following suggestion—not in an accusatory way, but in the same spirit we offer the other ideas in this book. If annual accumulation is easy for you, or if sending off an occasional check consistently adds up at year's end to what you wanted to give anyway, it is possible that you ought to consider challenging yourself to give more—to give an amount that would require sacrifices and continual effort on your part. Accumulation requires this kind of effort only when you have a truly challenging goal.

Dispersal

Prudent accumulation is largely dominated by one or two principles; dispersal, on the other hand, involves quite a few considerations. The difference lies in the fact that in accumulating money you are only preparing to have an effect, whereas in dispersing it you are creating at least as many effects as the number of organizations you support—and the wise steward wants to control every aspect of every effect.

The wise steward not only seeks to support the most effective and efficient groups; he also seeks to make them more effective and efficient through his support of them. From this goal arise two tactics for effective dispersal:

1. See that your gift to a given organization arrives at the same time each year, because a gift of any significant size affects cash flow, and you aid their cash-flow planning by being predictable.

2. See that as few gifts as possible arrive during the month of December. Why? Because "everyone" gives in December. Parachurch ministries receive as much as fifty percent of their income during what is the last month of most people's tax year. As a result, staff personnel are working (and overworking) frantically then; some ministries may even have to add seasonal help. Don't be the source of that one final check that forces them to hire temporary employees—and thus increases their costs.

This matter of timing can have a broad and significant impact. True, if only you and a small number of other stewards are carefully regulating your gifts, the effect might be insignificant. But the goal is to encourage a substantial number of stewards to give more uniformly and predictably. If this happens, the results will be impressive: the income of entire organizations will be distributed more evenly over the twelve-month period, enabling them to do better financial planning and to better control overhead.

The key to maximum coordination of accumulation and dispersal lies in *planned dispersal*. In planned dispersal, you begin your stewardship year (usually corresponding to the calendar year) by listing your proposed gifts, noting the order in which you will make them and the size of each. What you have done in the previous year probably determines this list. Perhaps you are a steward newly convinced of the value of investigation and have just finished gathering information about potential recipients, or perhaps you are an experienced steward thoroughly committed to a carefully selected list of six to ten recipients. Whatever your situation, the pattern is this: you accumulate funds until you have enough for the first gift, and then you give it. In this way you give systematically to every organization on your list, adopting the giving order from the previous year if it still reflects your commitment.

Maximum coordination of accumulation and dispersal may not be a realistic goal for every steward, however, because use of a dispersal list may be more a hindrance than a help for some. Those who know their income for the coming year — within, say, five percent — will find the list a valuable tool, because they can quite accurately forecast accumulation and total giving in advance. (Obviously, this presupposes that you are giving a predetermined percentage of income. If you're giving "off the top" as we advocate, you will need to rely on some kind of predetermining factor.)

When you cannot accurately forecast your income, the resulting difficulty lies not in compiling your list, but in determining the size of each gift. For those who have this difficulty, but who might still want to use a dispersal list in order to disperse money uniformly over a twelve-month period, we offer three approaches to the problem:

1. Prioritize the list. In other words, list organizations in order of importance, putting the organization you are most committed to first (probably your own church), and maintaining that pattern. Then put an amount next to each name on the list that represents what you will give if your income turns out to be the figure you have estimated. What you are then saying to yourself is, "I'm not going to give organizations lower on the list anything until I've accumulated X dollars for number one, Y dollars for number two . . . ," and so on.

2. Delay sending any gifts until you can quite accurately estimate your income for the year (but don't delay putting money aside).

3. Send donations to your entire list quarterly or semi-annually. This is the alternative we least recommend, because we're sure that most organizations would prefer receiving and processing one large gift of unpredictable size rather than several smaller gifts of predictable size.

As a final note on this subject, we want to admit to you, our reader, what you might already be thinking: that accumulation and dispersal are a complicated business. Yes, it's easy to get tangled up in their many details — but shouldn't they be considered at least as important as the many other financial transactions we make daily, like paying bills? Aren't they at least as important as our temporal investments?

Yet we don't want our enthusiasm for careful stewardship to suggest that we think a properly articulated accumulation and dispersal procedure must be written out like a corporate policy manual. If you have a clear mental picture of your plan, there's no need to write it down. But actually remembering to send the money out at the ideal time challenges even the steward with the sharpest memory. For this reason it's often best to put dispersal reminders on a calendar, or devise some other means of red-lettering important dates. Looking things over briefly each time you make a deposit in your stewardship checking account is another means of staying aware of your commitments.

Our third stone in a solidly founded stewardship program is a careful defining of your *stewardship interests*, and then a focusing of those interests. Without this you will either find it impossible to limit yourself to six to ten recipients — or you will select recipients sheerly at random. Some readers may be alarmed by this emphasis on *their interests* in giving, rather than on God's will. But we believe that the two are related, not opposed. God gives you these interests; they are stimulants to your concern, and, as such, they encourage you to give. In fact, it is a tribute to God's love and thoughtfulness that he directs our stewardship by giving us interests in various areas of the work of the Great Commission. If we follow and develop these interests, they can add to our joy in giving.

To define your interests, take time to sit down and think about them carefully, discussing them with your spouse if you're married. Identify your interests clearly and think about them long enough to discover which ones matter most — and therefore have priority. Here's an idea for getting started on the definition of your interests. Without doing any previous reflection, sit down and begin to pray about Christian work anywhere and everywhere. The activities and groups that come to mind most quickly are valuable indications of your interests. When thinking this way you should be aware of the different categories into which stewardship interests may be grouped: geographical, cultural, and functional. Organizations can also be grouped according to effectiveness and efficiency. Bear in mind that these are not a set of mutually exclusive categories leading to an exhaustive list of interests; rather, they are a series of alternative perspectives.

Some stewards, feeling that people everywhere are equally needy (from a spiritual point of view), support the organizations they find to be most effective and efficient. Other people's highest priority is the support of a particular individual or individuals. They usually develop a strong allegiance in this situation, supporting whatever the mission and whatever the ministry.[1] But most people have interests that fall into the first three categories — geographically, culturally, or functionally related interests. And thanks be to God that he has given one a strong interest in Africa and another in China; that one is primarily interested in home missions and another in telling the Word to primitive "unreached" peoples; that one has a passion for church planting and another for evangelism. All the work must be done — and variety in interests is primary insurance that it will be done.

In order to stimulate your thinking about your interests, we have compiled three lists that flesh out the categories mentioned above. Again we add that these lists are by no means exhaustive.

Many stewards' interests center on people in particular cultural situations or comprising a particular cultural group:

- the poor and culturally disadvantaged
- peoples of particular world religions and sects
- people in the various racially-based sub-cultures within our society
- "unreached" peoples living in primitive areas
- people in other western nations
- citizens of Communist bloc nations
- people of other developed nations
- people of developing nations
- students
- foreign students studying in the Unites States
- armed forces personnel
- children
- businessmen and women
- housewives
- people in a particular industry or profession
- athletes

[1]Admirable as we think this kind of commitment is, we feel we should include a legal note here. If the individual you're supporting joins an organization whose performance you find wanting and would not otherwise support, you should be aware of this IRS ruling: that contributions that are termed "fully designated" — gifts that the donor insists go to the support of the designee — are *not* tax deductible. In addition, should your friend's support be oversubscribed, you will then, in effect, be supporting the organization itself — and with a non-deductible gift.

Other stewards are interested in people in particular geographical areas:

- home missions (USA & Canada)
- Latin America:
  - Central America
  - South America
- Europe
- The Middle East
- Africa
  - Northern Africa
  - Eastern Africa
  - Western Africa
  - Southern Africa
- Asia
  - the Indian sub-continent
  - Japan
  - Korea
  - China
  - Southeast Asia
  - the islands of the Pacific

Still others are interested in particular types of ministry with specific functions:

- evangelism
- church planting
- literature
- translation
- relief and development
- medicine
- service and support:
  - transportation
  - technology
  - coordination and cooperation
- education
  - Christian schooling (including Bible schools and seminaries)
  - literary training
  - counseling

Naturally, as you pick and choose according to your strongest interests, you may find that you make a few choices in each category. We would think this would be the case for most readers. And we hope that these lists are helpful to you, because they represent just about all the concrete help we can offer on this subject. It's basically your job to define your stewardship interests at this point. Before you begin, however, here is one important caution: do *not* attempt to exhaustively identify every last interest you have. Most people, taking stock of themselves in the less meticulous manner we have suggested, identify somewhere between six and ten interests (including their own church)—and this is the ideal number. If the number of your interests doesn't fall within this range, remember that it's better to have less than six interests than to try to support more than ten of them.

This is probably an appropriate place to defend our assertion about the proper number of recipients, which should be no more than ten. You should limit yourself to this number because, unless you can devote most or all of your time to stewardship, this is as many interests — and recipients — as you can effectively keep up with. The key word here is *effectively*; keep in mind that *thorough* stewardship is a time-consuming matter. As we have pointed out earlier, you need to select the recipients on the basis of thorough knowledge, which means sending for answers to detailed questions, not simply looking over the limited information that organizations send you. Once you have made your selection, you will be responsible for praying for these organizations regularly. And, finally, you need to responsibly *maintain* your interests in these recipients by frequently requesting additional and updated information. All this takes time.

Remember, too, that each of your annual gifts should be large enough to be meaningful to you — a real stimulus to your continued concern for the groups receiving them. Supporting too many organizations means sending a plethora of small gifts that will probably diminish that sense of purpose.

Of course, by saying this we are not suggesting that you toss out your current list of recipients and start over again. We are, however, advocating what is probably a rather significant change in your approach to deciding who will receive your money. To go from a subjective viewpoint (determined completely by your interests) to an objective viewpoint (determined by your assessment of which organizations will best serve your interests) will require a careful decision-making process that should be based on the best information you can obtain.

You need to take two logical steps to obtain this information. The first step is the Who's Who side of things: locating listings of qualified candidates. The second step is obtaining the factual and financial details about groups that work in your areas of interest. Most of the remainder of this book deals, in detail, with the successful execution of this selection process.

The next chapter, which describes informative sources, is a sort of reference guide to the various methods of collecting information. But before moving on, we need to add two more supports to our solid foundation for giving.

The next important factor is, in fact, the primary theme of this book: *knowing your recipient*. This is a *perpetual* process: the steps we discuss immediately above should be only the beginning of a *steady* flow of information between your recipients and you, because as long as support money is flowing *from* you, information affirming the recipient's continued qualification for that support should be flowing *to* you. And it is important to reiterate the point that, if you want the organization's full story, you will no doubt have to ask for supplementary information, and not rely only on the candidate's fund-raising materials. But we needn't say more about knowing your recipient here, because that will be our major topic hereafter.

Our remaining foundation stone is the one only the organizations themselves ever think much about: *maintaining commitment*. Only the best stewards have given more than a passing thought to the matter of the continuity and consistency of their support of chosen recipients. But this is a strategic matter that warrants attention and discussion.

The candidates for your support are obliged to furnish you with the information you require. If you choose to support them, they tacitly take on the additional obligation to keep you informed. But from the time they gain a place on your stewardship list, you have an obligation to them, too, as long as they merit your support. The essence of this obligation can be summed up in the word *commitment*. You ought to feel committed to your chosen recipients as long as they work responsibly in the areas of ministry that interest you. And it is important to realize that your commitment is a very real part of your support: they need to know that they can count on you. You maintain your commitment—and demonstrate it—by two means: *continuity* and *consistency*.

Consistency involves timing, a factor strategic to successful cash-flow management within the organizations you support. Your *annual* gift (remember that a single large gift per year is easiest for them to process) should reach the recipient at the same time each year—within the same month. The more an organization's support comes from committed donors making predictable gifts, the more efficient that organization can be. And you help maintain that efficiency (by easing the surprise) when you inform them of any change in your gift. One foreign missions fund-raiser told us that his organization is jolted whenever regular supporters shift from quarterly to annual giving, or vice versa, without announcing the change. The gift seems to have quadrupled or disappeared, depending on how the donor changed his giving pattern. So if you decide to alter the amount, timing, or frequency of a gift, advise the organization to be affected: send them a quick note, mailed separately or enclosed with the gift.

Continuity means an uninterrupted flow of support—in real dollars—at an established level. This involves two additional provisions:

1. *Making inflation adjustments:* Such adjustments, naturally, should come out of increases in *your* income created by inflation adjustments. Handling these adjustments can be simple: just assign to each of your recipients a percentage of your total giving. Then, as your income increases, their percentage of it increases accordingly. If your income is fixed, or at least unchanged, then no increase in size of gifts is called for. Conversely, if your income increases dramatically, nothing in your commitment requires that your present recipients receive a share of the complete increase. Only an inflation adjustment is in order.

2. *Providing a share in your estate:* We believe that the principle here is definitely *not* that money should continue flowing indefinitely to your recipients in fixed amounts and at fixed intervals. The recipients should instead be granted a portion of your estate, to be distributed, if possible, in *single* lump sums. Again, the idea here is to avoid "proliferation of gifts."

This discussion of the steward's responsibilities to the organizations he supports—viewed as a commitment—completes our analysis of the foundation of responsible stewardship. This discussion is pivotal: it marks our transition from the perspectives of the opening chapters to the prescriptions for action in the following chapters.

SOME BASIC BOOKS ON STEWARDSHIP

Berner, Carl W., Jr. *The Power of Pure Stewardship*. St. Louis, Missouri: Concordia Publishing House, 1970.

Brattgard, Helge. *God's Stewards*. Minneapolis, Minnesota: Augsburg Publishing House, 1963.

Kauffman, Milo. *Stewards of God*. Scottsdale, Pennsylvania: Herald Press, 1975.

Olford, Stephen. *The Grace of Giving*. Grand Rapids, Michigan: Zondervan Publishing House, 1972.

Rolston, Holmes. *Stewardship and the New Testament Church*. Richmond, Virginia: John Knox Press, 1948.

Werning, Waldo J. *The Stewardship Call*. St. Louis, Missouri: Concordia Publishing House, 1965.

CHAPTER SIX

USING SOURCES OF INFORMATION
SUCCESSFULLY

In this chapter we begin defining the actual process of improving our performance as stewards. Again, our basic premise is that we will decide whom to support on the basis of information we secure for that purpose. Of course, the question that immediately arises is, "Where can such information be obtained? What are the sources?"

As we indicated in the previous chapter, the answer is two-fold because there are logically two steps in the search: identification and evaluation. As our discussion will prove, these sources of information frequently overlap in function. The first of the two is logically prior. When some Christians set out to improve their performance as stewards, they begin by seeking information about the organizations of which they are already aware. Others, however, choose a more basic starting point, asking, "Who are the groups whose purposes reflect my stewardship interests?" This means beginning their search by accumulating the names of new organizations which become at that point only "candidates" for their support. In either case, the primary goal is identification.

Let's now take a look at several available sources, noting their potential for providing both descriptive and evaluative information. The most useful categorization of these sources is formal/informal or impersonal/personal. The formal sources are impersonal, the informal sources personal — and all sources fall somewhere along a formal/informal continuum. We'll begin at the far right of the continuum, discussing the most formal and impersonal source first: printed reference material.

By far and away the most helpful reference tool in print is a large cloth-bound book entitled *Mission Handbook: North*

American Protestant Ministries. Published periodically by the Missions Advanced Research and Communication Center in southern California, this book is impressive in scope: it provides details about 600 foreign missions headquartered in North America. Because it lists all agencies with which MARC has contact — and endorses or evaluates none — it is primarily a source of identifying information. (Of course, the membership listings of various associations are an endorsement of sorts, because the associations have significant membership requirements.) The *Mission Handbook* indexes these 600 agencies in each of the following ways:

- by primary task (function)
- by countries of service
- by membership in missions associations

Multiple references also make organizations easy to find. For example, you can look up all the countries that ABC Mission works in, *and* you can see all the groups working in country Z, which can be almost any country in the world. Similarly, you can look up all the function areas in which Mission ABC works, *and* you can see all the groups who work in functional areas X, Y, and Z. Also included in this book are a significant survey of mission events of the past two or three years, a directory of schools and professors of missions, and several other important features.

Getting your hands on this book is important if you're searching for information. Start by checking your church library. If it isn't there, it should be. You can purchase it at your bookstore or direct from the publisher. Write to:

MARC Publications
919 West Huntington Drive
Monrovia, California, 91016

The *Mission Handbook* is essentially the only reference source you need if you're gathering identifying information on foreign missions. But what about reference sources — or any printed sources — describing organizations doing work in North America? Here the picture does not focus so sharply.

Regrettably, there is no book like the *Mission Handbook* for North American missions. In addition, many of the groups seeking support for domestic ministry have goals and purposes that defy easy categorization. But you can use as guides the membership directories of various associations of ministries. An organization's membership in an association is a kind of endorsement — to the extent that the membership requirements are restrictive, and to the extent that those requirements make what you think are important distinctions. As such, membership lists can be used as sources of evaluative information. Good examples of such lists are the membership rolls of the National Association of Evangelicals; the American Association of Bible Colleges; the Association of Christian Schools, International (there are several other associations of Christian schools); the Association of North American Missions; and the Association of National Religious Broadcasters. The evaluation inherent in such lists has no gradations; it is strictly the "YES" half of a "YES/NO." Those organizations listed have satisfied the membership requirements; any unlisted have not. The thoughtful steward may conclude that he isn't interested in any group that doesn't meet such requirements. If so, the membership directories of such associations can provide him with valuable descriptive information.

But these reference items are not the only sources that come in printed form. There are more informal printed sources, too, such as the many journalistic publications available from evangelical publishers. One of the common — and most appropriate — running themes in these general-interest evangelical magazines is the fulfillment of the Great Commission. In these publications, everything from news coverage to personality features will be a natural source of descriptive information. Unfortunately, however, the amount of evaluative information available from this source is small. This is the case because many evangelicals oppose vigorous and responsive journalism within evangelicalism. At the core of this opposition is a myopic conviction that the believers should *never* hang their dirty linen in view of "the world." This is a sadly misguided belief. What we evangelicals need to develop instead is the conviction that we *must* have journalism so keen and responsive that the next time there is a Jonestown the world will not confuse the poor, gullible souls in the cult with evangelical Christians, and so dismiss them as "just another bunch of fundamentalists." It is those with whom the world confuses us — because we are so ineptly silent — that hurt our work the most. And, those influential people who strive to enforce the "no dirty linen" policy help create a related problem: the believers *themselves* don't know much about each other, either.

Lately, however, forthrightness seems to be gaining support, despite the unpleasantness it may bring for a season. The March 1977 issue of *Eternity* magazine bears this out: it carried an article on this matter, entitled "Non-Prophet Christian Journalism." And journalists at *Christianity Today* magazine have felt for some time that such writing was one of the duties of their calling. (Remember the article cited in Chapter 4 — "Korean Orphan Appeal: How Long?" written in 1972.) Their recent coverage of a running feud between two highly controversial Bible-smuggling operations behind the Iron Curtain met with powerful two-pronged opposition. First of all, the magazine's decision-makers faced the threat of significant legal costs, because their subjects were apparently willing to channel large portions of their revenues into legal actions against the magazine that would serve to divert the spotlight from their activities. Secondly, the magazine's leaders faced "dirty linen" opposition as close at hand as an occasional member or two of their own board of directors.* Journalists of less mettle would have quickly thrown up their hands in surrender — but these people didn't. Thanks to courageous efforts like these, the situation is improving, but the need for honesty is still great. The evangelical press will not be a significant source of evaluative information for us as long as *Christianity Today* and *Eternity* remain in the position of crusaders, even among their peers.

Our next source of information is incontestably unique. Though this source is certainly the easiest to use, it is known for the quantity — not the quality — of information it provides. As a result, it's strictly a source of descriptive information. It's a source you "consult" every day: your mailbox. To maximize the value of your mailbox as a source of information, try this:

*The magazine's board of directors has made a great deal of progress since this occurrence.

Accumulate, for a few months, all solicitations for funds that are sent to you. Then sit down some evening, separate from the total collection all those pieces devoted to raising funds for Christian work, and read (or at least skim) all of them, making comparisons and taking some notes. Essentially you will be looking for descriptive information. But, after a while, you will also be able to make some evaluative decisions based on who will go to what excess of emotional persuasion, and who will insist most emphatically on having the most imperative need for your money.

Beyond printed sources, the first source to consider is direct contact with the various associations of evangelical ministries. But before you attempt to use this source, you should know its particular values and limitations. First of all, each association is the primary source of its own membership list. The membership requirements of each group make their list an implied endorsement, as we said earlier. Secondly, the unique value of this source lies in what you may learn about non-members. If you want to know why a certain group is not a member of the association to which — on the basis of goals and function — they could belong, contact that association by phone or letter, and ask. For example, if you were to write the Interdenominational Foreign Mission Association and ask why the Wycliffe Translators are not members, IFMA Executive Director Jack Frizen would give this answer: "While Wycliffe is not a member of any evangelical association, the organization is well respected for the expertise of its dedicated workers in linguistics and Bible translation." But if you were to contact Frizen about a much less deserving group, you would be told something like, "Mission X is not a member of the IFMA because we have not received full information about its operation. Thus we are not able to recommend it as meeting the standards of the IFMA."

Men like Frizen, Wade Coggins of the Evangelical Foreign Mission Association, Billy Melvin of the National Association of Evangelicals, and others are probably somewhat familiar with any organization that can afford to send you a letter. And, while there are legal proscriptions and other restrictions governing how much information these men can pass along to you, none of them has grown callous to seeing good money pass into abusive and inefficient hands, and they will help you as much as they possibly can. The sort of information you will *not* get from these associations is that by which you could find one member more worthy of your support than another. This obviously is not the purpose of the associations, and any transmittal of this sort of information — if they do have it — would be highly detrimental to the association itself.

Still more personal and informal is the missions committee of your local church. Don't underestimate this source, especially if they are an aware group belonging to their own national association — the Association of Church Missions Committees, a group whose objectives closely parallel those described in this book. Naturally, because this book focuses on stewardship beyond the church, many readers will be surprised at this suggestion. But we recommend the missions committee to help you in a procedure called *transmittal*. With this procedure, you send gifts to the organizations of your choice (not included on the church's missions budget), but you do so *through* your church. You simply make out your check to your church, enclosing with it instructions that specify to whom the money should go. The church's check for that amount is then forwarded to the group you name.

Transmittal has many benefits to recommend it. First, your transmitted funds become part of the church's missions budget. In raising the total budget in this manner, you make it that much more accurate a picture of the congregation's total missions giving. A second benefit is that of information: the missions committee will most likely be willing to give you information they have indicating the worthiness of your choices. Very valuable would be a frank, relaxed discussion with knowledgeable missions committee members about the reputation and performance of organizations you support. Keep in mind, however, that when you ask questions like, "Who does a good job in such and such a ministry?" these people will only naturally emphasize organizations to which the church is presently committed.

Many people who know a great deal about securing information — especially modern journalists — would tell us that we have not yet touched on the most important source of all: person-to-person contact with knowledgeable people. These *should be* people you know, but they *must* be people who know what they're talking about. Why is it important that you know the person? Because that factor so often affects the quality of information you get. Someone who knows what you want to know about various organizations very often got that knowledge by being the sort of person who could be trusted with it. He or she is going to be careful whom they tell, and careful to learn what that person plans to do with the information. Of course, we're not dealing with state secrets here, but few people provide useful information of this sort to strangers. Another reason for familiarity is simple: you should be at least reasonably confident of the person whose information you accept — and that confidence demands knowing him.

An obvious first choice in such situations is a pastor who has proven worthy of your trust. If he has been trustworthy and helpful before, he will probably be a good source of advice about support of parachurch organizations. Very probably he will only tell you things about which he is quite certain, even at the expense of seeming not to know too much. And, like the missions committee, the pastor will find impartiality much easier if you ask him to evaluate organizations you bring up rather than to suggest some organizations. If he is asked to suggest possibilities, he will only naturally tend to mention groups that the church supports. This is especially true for a denominational pastor whose church supports denominational ministries.

A pastor quite naturally receives a continuing flow of useful information about various ministries through his relationships with other clergymen. In fact, of all the people you know, he is probably the best informed about parachurch ministries. Nevertheless, many readers of this book will know others equally well informed — or even better informed. Again, the same qualifications apply: your source should be someone you know, and someone who is knowledgeable. A caution about whom to avoid: Everyone knows people who like to gossip, who flavor what they do know with what they wish were true. In matters of this sort, it is best not to consult them.

One source of information remains. We have reviewed every commonly available source except this one — the organization itself. When you have done your identification work and have a list of candidates for your support, who better to ask than the candidates themselves? But the success of this tactic depends on knowing what information to request and how to assess it — two strategic skills that are the subject of the final three chapters.

• CHAPTER SEVEN •

MAKING YOUR INQUIRY EFFECTIVE

In this chapter we will discuss the best way to elicit helpful information from the organization itself. Before we begin, be assured of one thing about such an inquiry: you *will* have an effect. When you write a letter like the one we propose, you put yourself in very select company. Those who ask for information *of any kind* comprise less than twenty percent of all people with whom Christian ministries have fund-raising contact each year — including church missions committees and foundations. Quite naturally, a letter of this kind makes a significant impression on those receiving it. They tend to think of you as a steward who is unlikely to respond to the usual emotional appeal — one who is thoughtful and careful enough to recognize that Christian organizations vary greatly in ability and performance. They also recognize that such a steward gives significant amounts to a limited number of organizations that he approves of, so it's worth the time required to answer his letter.

Unfortunately, what the letter won't do is separate the sheep from the goats. It will evoke the same image in the minds of those groups who like to hear from careful stewards as it does in the minds of those who prefer their donors to be somewhat less discerning. Because your letter implicitly tells them you're more aware of what's going on, and that you give more when you do give, you are going to get very cordial, very carefully worded personal letters in return. But the responses from those who appreciate the opportunity to answer and from those who respond only to save face won't differ perceptibly in tone or appearance — only in the substance and kind of information given.

The letter we propose asks for information about five basic

things: doctrinal position, goals and purposes, leadership, finances, and future plans. Rather than asking questions, it requests statements, because many of these statements are already prepared in traditional formats and can be easily released in response — *if* the organization is cooperative. In a typical letter we state our requests as follows:

Please send us:

1. Your doctrinal statement.
2. Your statement of purpose. Please include some information on successful past fulfillment of these purposes.
3. A complete list of the names of your officers and board of directors.
4. The financial statement released by your organization for the latest complete fiscal year, and, if possible, for the two previous fiscal years, also. Please include a copy of the auditor's cover letter if your statement is audited.
5. Key future plans for your program: special projects and, especially, permanent projects.

There is nothing sacrosanct about these five requests. They are not the only possible areas of inquiry, not the only worthwhile ones. But these five requests do help you cover the essential bases, yet are brief enough to help you avoid getting a discouraging, skimpy reply. And they do represent a consensus: they are the questions most often asked by people who are serious Christian stewards.

Our files contain scores of such letters of request that we have sent over the years — certainly more than a careful steward would need to send. But here we want to concentrate on two particular letters, each sent to thirty-six different organizations and designed to provide survey results that could be summarized in this book. Drawing on our years of experience with organizations of this type, we strategically composed the list of thirty-six to include three basic kinds of groups: those we thought would comply enthusiastically, others that would simply comply, and still others that would supply only part of the information or would not reply at all. We did in fact get all of these responses, but not without a number of surprises. Actually, the responses to the letters constitute two surveys, because a two-year interval separated the sending of each letter, and each organization involved was queried twice. The first letter was sent in April and June of 1978; the second letter was sent in August 1980. We used these two stages to determine how much (if at all) disclosure habits were changing. We found the results very interesting, and we think you will, too.

Our survey has proven all the more interesting because it comes during an especially significant era in the history of fund-raising by parachurch organizations,[1] at a time when the matter of organizations acknowledging their responsibilities to their constituencies is a very vital question. A particular issue these days is what constitutes sufficient financial disclosure. From several sides the parachurch groups are being pressured to disclose more complete information. Some of the recent pressure has been threatening: in 1977, for example, the U. S. Congress seemed ready to vote into law certain measures (Bill HR 41) aimed at all non-profit groups — measures that were exceedingly broad and extensively demanding. To many observers the bill seemed more likely to hurt than to help. Fortunately, the legislation was not passed, and this threat appears to have lessened — for the time being, at least. But this pressure has produced some positive results: soon after the HR-41 threat, members of the larger and more responsible associations of parachurch groups meaningfully strengthened their financial disclosure requirements. An excellent example is the work done by the Accounting Task Force of the Interdenominational Foreign Mission Association with the membership of that association. Denominational groups have also played a significant role in effecting broader financial disclosure.

But perhaps the most notable result of the pressure for more thorough disclosure was the formation of a new and important "watchdog" organization within the evangelical ranks: the Evangelical Council for Financial Accountability. The ECFA was begun with a meeting held in Chicago in the fall of 1977. Two years later, the association had been formed, a board of direc-

---

[1]The reader will probably notice the names of a number of denominationally related organizations on our survey list; we did contact a number of such organizations.

tors had been chosen, and the processing of membership applications had begun. The ECFA and similar groups have goals much like those of the authors of this book. They realize, as we do, that currently there are both sheep and goats in the large number of organizations that refuse to divulge financial information. They want to separate the worthy organizations from the unworthy by encouraging them to be financially frank. And they encourage this separation as much to identify the unworthy as to protect the worthy.

So far, the ECFA has had a remarkable effect. It is beginning to drive a wedge between the honorable parachurch organizations and those less than honest. This wedge has not completely separated the sheep from the goats . . . yet. That will come later — to the glory of God — when resistance to these reforms is exhausted. But the wedge has separated the diehard nondisclosers from those who have said, "OK, we see the light. You're welcome to the data we have, and we'll get an audit to verify our figures." The ECFA is successful because its leadership is struggling to be honest, not building a facade or playing games for appearance's sake. Organizations that do not fulfill the requirements are being refused membership, and each member must reapply and resatisfy the requirements each year. As a result, many parachurch groups are doing an about-face on their financial disclosure policies. And, even more important, the ECFA is not reticent about observing the conduct of members to see if they are upholding the association's regulations. Because both Edward Hales, co-author of this book, and Donald Mortenson, our chief adviser on Chapter 9, are members of the ECFA Standards Committee, we have been in close touch with ECFA headquarters for some time. In fact, Executive Director Olan Hendrix and his staff have been very diligent in requesting information from us on the infractions of ECFA rules, by member organizations, that our survey uncovered.

Two incidents from our first survey will illustrate how much — and how suddenly — disclosure policies are changing, often because of the ECFA's influence. The ECFA is like an evangelist: it doesn't convert everyone, but it makes everyone decide.

The first incident involves an organization that refused us financial data in a most diplomatic manner — we received a telephone call from the regional development (i.e., fund-raising) representative. He offered to bring the financial statements to a meeting, but he would not leave the data in our possession. We did not feel this offer truly complied with our request, and we did not want to weaken our survey results by treating one group differently from the rest. As we were wondering what to do next, the field representative called again, announcing that he had conferred with his boss, and could now offer to leave the statements with us for 48 hours. We were quite impressed: here was a director of development and his field man living with the (somewhat antiquated) dictates of their superiors but bending them enough to adapt to the changing environment of stewardship. They probably figured that, with the help of a Xerox machine, we could easily copy the information we needed within forty-eight hours — and they were right. The field representative later informed us that his organization was planning to begin full disclosure, but "not yet." It was probably from these plans that he and his superior drew their room to maneuver.

The second vignette from our first survey involves one of those groups with an "exchange" relationship with their supporters, the kind of relationship that we discuss in Chapter 3: they raise money from the same audience to whom they minister. Possibly because of this advantage, they apparently had become used to having their way. Their response included only their doctrinal statement, board membership list, and statement of purpose. The package contained only one printed piece: the doctrinal statement. The other two pieces of information were included in their letter of reply to us. Following these items in the letter came a one-paragraph comment on their failure to enclose financial information. With a curt finality likely born of years of commitment to the "right" of privacy in these matters, that paragraph stated,

> We regret that we do not have a financial statement that is distributed. The only one we have available is the CPA auditor's report which is made up for the board of directors and is too detailed for the average layman to understand.

But then, as if wanting to close on a more positive note, they added: "If there is any further information you may need, please do not hesitate to let us know."

We had determined in advance that it would be our policy *not* to recontact the organizations surveyed to obtain more information than they would part with through their first response, because that would put any groups not recontacted at a disadvantage. However, we decided to make this refusal (the first) a test case of our ability to obtain financial information about the group through their IRS form 990 (Return of Organization Exempt from Income Tax), on file with the Internal Revenue Service. Having reached this decision, we felt it our first duty to inform the ministry in question of our determination not to be dissuaded by their refusal. After briefly describing his background and familiarity with financial materials, Mr. Youngren said in a letter to them:

> . . . Let me assure you that I would much rather gain my financial orientation to your work through your own statement than through your form 990 . . . but that the latter is readily available to me through form 4605.
>   Allow me to thank you in advance for your careful attention to this matter.

This declaration of our intent drew no response, so we went ahead with our plans.

Now, as the reader may know, to approach the IRS with anything save one's tax return and payment is to experience the powerlessness of being "man" in the contest of man and the bureaucratic monster. (Our point here is not ineptitude in the bureaucracy, but the sheer mystery of the experience.) We started by calling two IRS offices in our own area of the country, metropolitan Chicago. At the end of each conversation — invariably unproductive — we would ask the name of the person to whom we were speaking so that we would have an entree at the time of our next call. It did no good. After six weeks of this sort of thing, we became convinced that no one willing to come to the phone or approach a reception desk at either of these offices knew any more than we did about obtaining a 990 from the file. At that point we briefly stopped our efforts —

until a *rumor* (nothing more) pointed us to Philadelphia. We were in the process of contacting the main office in Philadelphia by telephone and letter when, suddenly, the monster moved. And it did not move to avoid us — it moved toward us, and revealed, with memorable specificity, exactly what we wanted to know.

The phone rang at 7:20 a.m., reaching Alan Youngren at breakfast. Even though that was 8:20 in Philadelphia, from whence the call came, it still seemed impressive. Without offering name, rank, or serial number, and referring to our inquiries with little beyond inference, the caller assured Mr. Youngren that this was going to be a breakthrough for him. He then backed up this assertion with an eight-item IRS address for the Cincinnati office, including a nine-digit reference number. He went on to point out that the great detail of this address would reveal — to those inside the IRS — not only the route of the correct office mail cart, but the precise desk on which to put the letter.

We immediately mailed the proper paper, and in twelve days we had the 990 in our hands. The only national event with which we can possibly correlate our amazing turn of fortune is the off-year election (of 1978), a time when wise bureaucrats reach the zenith of their biennial cycle of responsiveness. Remarkable as all this was, a greater surprise — and the real spoils of victory — came three days later when we heard from our contact at the organization whose 990 we had secured. It had been seven-and-a-half months since our last contact, but the letter began, "I am happy to respond to your inquiry requesting a financial statement"; enclosed was a condensed statement for the 1977 fiscal year.

A final note on this second story. Our request reached the IRS approximately one month prior to an extended deadline for this ministry's filing of its 990 for fiscal 1978. Apparently because they knew we didn't have the 990 for 1978, they didn't volunteer that information. They gave us only what they knew we had, still clinging to all the privacy they could maintain. How they learned of our success in finally obtaining their 990 for 1977 — and learned of it so soon after the fact — we will probably never know. We trust that our including this story will give our reader an impression of the potency of his power to obtain the 990 report, but also of the blessing that is his if he doesn't have to endure the process of doing so.

The ultimate point here is that, in both of these instances, the ECFA played a part in the unpredictable and varying responses we received. Certainly it drove a wedge between the ostensibly cooperative organization and the organization whose 990 we obtained. Our second survey bears this out: in it, one of the two groups turned around and gave us three years' worth of financial data, exemplary in every way; the other group never responded. The crowning irony is that the group that resisted to the end in "round one" gave us the full data the second time, but the group with the helpful development director was mute.

We recount these experiences only to show you what *can* happen. And before we present a summary of the results of our survey, we want to follow strong dictates of conscience as well as common sense by stating one caution very plainly: You, our reader, should not take *our* experience as a basis for your conclusions; no group in this survey has refused *you* information. Remember that many organizations have begun disclosing financial data since our survey was completed. You should therefore formulate your conclusions only on the basis of what you receive — or don't receive — in response to your own inquiries. We wrote this set of seventy-two letters for the purposes of this book, and of course we want the responses to be an example of the sort of results that will be obtained from such inquiries. But we think it entirely inappropriate for anyone to use this survey to draw conclusions about the disclosure policies of any parachurch organizations, especially in light of the changes taking place in such disclosure.

Of particular value to you, we believe, is the scope of our survey. It gives you a big picture that you won't get by writing for information from the groups that interest you (unless you're tremendously ambitious and send out scores of inquiries). When you get a reply to an inquiry of your own that surprises you for some reason, our survey may show you just how surprising — or predictable — that reply really is. You might, for example, hear from XYZ Ministry in just four days, and wonder how prompt a response that is. For an answer, check the time-to-reply column in our survey summary. (We note the time that each group took to respond to each survey.) When you do, you'll notice that we heard from Trinity Evangelical Divinity School in two days, an astounding 48 hours — certainly the equivalent, in "post haste," of a hole-in-one. And then you can check the other sixty-four reply times[2] to get an accurate picture of the norm.

Finally, we include a quick description of the survey that follows:

For the doctrinal statement, the statement of purpose, and the statement of future plans, we note whether the statement was furnished, and whether it was pre-printed, photocopied, or typed in answer to our inquiry.

In summarizing the board of directors listing and the financial statement, we go into more detail. For the listing of directors we note, in addition, the following: [3]

1. If indicated, the estimated percent of the board composed of employees and/or family,

2. If possible, a rough estimation of the proportion of U.S. geography represented by board members' areas of residence.

3. If, for each non-employee board member, the listing gives his profession and/or professional connection (names the organization he or she is affiliated with).

4. If, for each non-employee board member, the listing gives his state of residence.

For the financial statement, we answer even more questions:

1. Was it provided?
2. Is it a CPA-audited statement?
3. If so, was the CPA's covering (opinion) letter enclosed, as requested?
4. Is the statement a "complete report," as defined in Chapter 9?

[2] The figure is not "seventy-two" because seven organizations did not respond.

[3] For a discussion of the value of the items, see Chapter 8.

5. How many years' data were supplied? (three were requested)

6. If there is a CPA audit involved, is the CPA's letter for the latest year an "unqualified" letter, as defined in Chapter 9?

With a renewed request that you use this information only as a point of reference for your own inquiries, we present a summary of our survey results, along with a sample of our inquiry letter from each of the surveys.

NOTE: In order to meet publication deadlines, we had to establish a cutoff date for responses to the second survey (109 days after mailing our inquiry letters). However, we didn't need a cutoff date for the first survey. For this reason several response times in the first survey are higher than any in the second.

LEGEND:
X = Affirmative, material supplied
L = Material supplied in cover letter
Z = CPA letter gives no opinion
P = Photocopy (not pre-printed)
S = Some (partial) information supplied
Ind. = Indeterminable
# = Not relevant here: The AICPA guidelines for educational institutions do not demand the "complete report" we requested.

LETTER FOR FIRST SURVEY

J. Alan Youngren

June 15, 1978

Director of Stewardship

Dear Sir,

As part of an effort toward responsible stewardship of the financial means which God has entrusted to me, I am seeking information on your organization and its goals.

An important element of my consideration will be your responses to the series of inquiries I make below. These are intended as a means of gaining some familiarity with your organization's work.

I do not wish to take any more of your time in answering than is absolutely necessary. Please feel free to respond with any pre-printed materials you have which contain the information I am requesting. However, please make an adequate response to all five inquiries.

My information requests are as follows:

1. Your doctrinal statement.
2. Your statement of purpose. Please include some information on successful past fulfillment of these purposes.
3. A complete list of the names of your officers and board of directors.
4. The financial statement released by your organization for the latest complete fiscal year, and, if possible, for the two previous fiscal years also. Please include a copy of the auditor's cover letter, if your statement is audited.
5. Key future plans for your program: special projects, and, especially, permanent projects.

Thank you very much for your cooperation in this matter. I am enclosing a stamped, self-addressed envelope, and I await your reply with interest.

Very sincerely,

Alan Youngren

ORGANIZATION	RESPONSE TIME No. of Days	FUTURE PLANS Pre-printed	FUTURE PLANS Provided	FINANCIAL STATEMENT Is latest letter unqualified?	FINANCIAL STATEMENT No. years provided	FINANCIAL STATEMENT Complete report	FINANCIAL STATEMENT CPA letter	FINANCIAL STATEMENT CPA audit	FINANCIAL STATEMENT Provided	BOARD LIST Residence	BOARD LIST Profession	BOARD LIST Employer	BOARD LIST Est. % of U.S. geography covered	BOARD LIST Est. % who are relatives and employees	BOARD LIST Pre-printed	BOARD LIST Provided	STATEMENT OF PURPOSE Pre-printed	STATEMENT OF PURPOSE Provided	DOCTRINAL STATEMENT Pre-printed	DOCTRINAL STATEMENT Provided
Africa Inland Mission (American Council)	17	L	X	X	2	X	X	X	X	X	X	X	5%	30%	P	X	X	X	X	X
American Leprosy Mission	6	P	X	X	3	X	X	X	X	X	X	X	100%	0%	X	X	X	X	Have none	Have none
Good News Broadcasters (Back-to-the-Bible Broadcast)	30	P	X	X	3	No	X	X	X	—	—	—	—	100%	P	X	X	X	X	X
Bethel College & Seminary (Minnesota)	10	—	No	—	2	#	No	No	X	X	No	No	50%	0%	P	X	P	X	X	X
Bible Memory Association Int.	7	L	X	No	2	X	X	X	X	X	No	No	70%	14%	P	X	P	X	X	X
Bibles for the World	45	—	No	No	2	X	X	X	X	No	No	No	Ind.	40%	X	X	X	X	X	X
Campus Crusade for Christ	118	X	X	X	2	X	X	X	X	X	X	X	70%	25%	X	X	X	X	X	X
CAM International (formerly Central American Mission)	15	—	No	—	3	—	No	No	X	X	X	No	20%	35%	X	X	P	X	P	X
The Chapel of the Air	6	X	X	—	1	—	No	No	X	—	—	—	—	100%	X	X	X	X	X	X
Child Evangelism Fellowship	11	L	X	N	1	No	X	No	X	X	No	X	100%	5%	P	X	P	X	X	X
Compassion, Inc.	15	—	No	No	2	X	X	X	X	No	No	No	Ind.	25%	P	X	P	X	P	X
The Evangelical Alliance Mission (TEAM)												DID NOT RESPOND								
Fellowship of Christian Athletes	36	L	X	X	3	X	X	X	X	No	No	No	Ind.	7%	X	X	X	X	X	X

Organization											%							No.
Greater Europe Mission	X	X	—	X	X	No	No	No	X	X	35%	—	X	X	No	X	L	15
Holy Land Christian Mission	X	X	—	X	X	X	X	X	X	X	10%	No	X	X	X	No	—	27
Robert Schuller Ministries (Hour of Power)	No	—	No	No	No	No	—	—	No	S	—	—	No	No	No	No	—	166
International Students, Inc.	X	X	X	X	X	X	X	S	X	X	7%	P	X	X	X	X	X	145
Mission Aviation Fellowship	X	P	X	P	X	X	X*	No	X	No	38%	L	X	P	X	Z	X	10
Moody Bible Institute	X	X	X	X	X	—	—	X	—	X	7%	X	X	X	X	—	X	18
Northern Baptist Theological Seminary	X	X	No	P	X	#	X	X	X	No	15%	P	X	X	X	No	P	23
The Old Time Gospel Hour (Jerry Falwell)	P	No	—	No	—	—	—	No	No	No	—	—	No	No	No	—	—	22
Overseas Crusades	X	X	X	No	X	X	X	X	X	X	33%	No	X	X	X	X	L	14
Radio Bible Class	X	X	L	L	X	—	—	No	No	No	50%	L	X	No	X	No	—	10
Revival Fires Ministry	X	X	No	X	No	No	No	No**	X	X	10% Ind.	X	X	No	X	No	—	16
Slavic Gospel Association				DID NOT RESPOND														
OSFO International (The T. L. Osborn Fdn.)	No	L	No	No	—	—	—	—	No	No	—	—	No	No	No	—	—	22
Tom Skinner Associates	X	L	X	X	X	X	X	X	X	X	40%	X	X	X	X	L	X	43
Trans-World Radio	X	X	X	X	No	X	No	X	X	No	Ind.	X	X	X	X	Z	X	8
Trinity Evangelical Divinity School	P	P	X	X	X	#	X	X	X	X	8%	P	X	X	X	X	L	3
Unevangelized Fields Mission	X	P	No	No	X	X	—	—	—	—	—	—	No	X	No	No	—	11
Underground Evangelism	X	X	X	X	X	No	No	—	—	X	100%	X	X	No	No	No	—	5
Voice of China & Asia Missionary Society, Inc.	X	—	X	No	No	No	X	X	X	No	Ind.	X	X	No	X	Z	—	6

FIRST SURVEY

ORGANIZATION	DOCTRINAL STATEMENT — Provided	DOCTRINAL STATEMENT — Pre-printed	STATEMENT OF PURPOSE — Provided	STATEMENT OF PURPOSE — Pre-printed	BOARD LIST — Provided	BOARD LIST — Pre-printed	BOARD LIST — Est. % who are relatives and employees	BOARD LIST — Est. % of U.S. geography covered	BOARD LIST — Employer	BOARD LIST — Profession	BOARD LIST — Residence	FINANCIAL STATEMENT — Provided	FINANCIAL STATEMENT — CPA audit	FINANCIAL STATEMENT — CPA letter	FINANCIAL STATEMENT — Complete report	FINANCIAL STATEMENT — No. years provided	FINANCIAL STATEMENT — Is latest letter unqualified?	FUTURE PLANS — Provided	FUTURE PLANS — Pre-printed	RESPONSE TIME — No. of Days
World Evangelism (Morris Cerullo)	X	P	X	X	X	P	2%	100%	No	No	X	X	No	No	No	2	—	X	X	50
World Missionary Evangelism	X	L	X	L	No	—	—	—	—	—	—	No	—	—	—	—	—	No	—	29
World Opportunities	X	X	X	X	X	X	Ind.	Ind.	No	No	No	X	No	No	No	1	—	X	L	7
Youth for Christ	X	P	X	P	X	P	40%	100%	X	X	X	X	No	No	No	1	—	X	L	23

*An unusual problem of interpretation exists with this group. They do much overseas accounting, and they are uncommonly scrupulous in their disclosure, as is their CPA. Several other CPA letters we received called the same situation an audit. We have designated this a partial audit. (See Chapter Nine for a thorough discussion of audits and their significance.)

**Despite the GAAS/GAAP language of the letter covering this report, it is clearly an incomplete report, having only revenue and expense figures. A clean (or qualified) opinion on an incomplete report like this one is termed a piecemeal opinion, and piecemeal opinions no longer constitute acceptable auditing practice.

LETTER FOR SECOND SURVEY

August 4, 1980

marilyn novak

Director of Stewardship

Dear Sir,

My husband and I are committed to effective stewardship. In light of that commitment, I am writing to request certain information regarding your institution.

So that we may become more familiar with your work, please respond to five specific inquiries, as follows:

1. The names of your officers and your directors' board.

2. Your financial statement for the most recent completed fiscal year, and also, if possible, for the two fiscal years preceding that. If your statement is audited, please include the auditor's letter.

3. Your statement of faith.

4. A summary of your goals and purposes, and whatever comment you wish to include on successes in accomplishment of those purposes.

5. Plans for the future, especially undertakings which are new to your ministry.

While I am vitally interested in receiving adequate response to all five inquiries, it is also my intention that your response require as little time of you and your staff as possible, so feel free to send printed items or copies of previously written material.

Thank you most kindly for your attention to this request.

Very cordially,

Marilyn Novak

ORGANIZATION	Doctrinal Statement: Provided	Doctrinal Statement: Pre-printed	Statement of Purpose: Provided	Statement of Purpose: Pre-printed	Board List: Provided	Board List: Pre-printed	Board List: Est. % who are relatives and employees	Board List: Est. % of U.S. geography covered	Board List: Employer	Board List: Profession	Board List: Residence	Financial Statement: Provided	Financial Statement: CPA audit	Financial Statement: CPA letter	Financial Statement: Complete report	Financial Statement: No. years provided	Financial Statement: Is latest letter unqualified?	Future Plans: Provided	Future Plans: Pre-printed	Response Time: No. of Days
Africa Inland Mission (American Council)	X	P	X	X	X	X	15%	5%	No	No	X	X	X	X	No	3	X	X	X	36
American Leprosy Mission	Have none	Have none	X	X	X	X	0	100%	No	No	X	X	X	X	X	2	X	No	—	3
Good News Broadcasters (Back-to-the-Bible Broadcast)	X	X	X	X	X	X	40%	Ind.	No	No	No	X	No	No	No	3	No	X	X	21
Bethel College & Seminary (Minnesota)	X	X	X	X	X	X	0	35%	X	X	X	X	X	X	#	1	X	No	—	3
Bible Memory Association Int.	X	X	No	—	X	P	Ind.	75%	No	No	X	X	X	X	X	1	No	No	—	106
Bibles for the World	X	X	X	X	X	P	15%	20%	X	X	X	X	X	X	X	1	X	X	L	16
Campus Crusade for Christ	X	X	X	X	X	X	11%	70%	X	X	X	X	X	X	X	2	X	X	X	9
CAM International (formerly Central American Mission)	X	X	X	X	X	X	30%	20%	No	No	X	X	X	X	X	1	No	X	L	10
The Chapel of the Air	X	X	X	X	X	X	42%	Ind.	No	No	No	X	No	No	No	1	—	No	—	5
Child Evangelism Fellowship	X	X	X	L	X	No	Ind.	Ind.	No	No	No	X	X	X	X	3	X	X	L	12
Compassion, Inc.	X	X	X	X	X	X	25%	25%	X	X	X	X	X	X	X	1	X	X	X	12
The Evangelical Alliance Mission (TEAM)	X	X	X	X	X	P	5%	20%	X	X	No	X	X	X	X	2	X	No	—	3
Fellowship of Christian Athletes	X	P	P	P	X	P	0	100%	No	No	X	X	X	X	X	2	No	No	—	18

Organization	1	2	3	4	5	6	7	8	9	10	11	12	13	14
Greater Europe Mission	X	X	32%	Ind.	No	No	X	X	X	3	X	X	L	4
Holy Land Christian Mission	X	X	42%	Ind.	No	No	X	X	X	1	X	X	L	21
Robert Schuller Ministries (Hour of Power)	X	No	20%	60%	X	X	X	No	No	1	X	X	L	30
International Students, Inc.	DID NOT RESPOND													
Mission Aviation Fellowship	X	X	16%	Ind.	X	No	X	No	No	3	Z	No	—	12
Moody Bible Institute	DID NOT RESPOND													
Northern Baptist Theological Seminary	X	No	0	Ind.	No	No	X	X	X	3	No	X	X	9
The Old Time Gospel Hour (Jerry Falwell)	P	X	50%	Ind.	No	No	X	X	#	3	X	No	—	48
Overseas Crusades	X	X	18%	Ind.	X	No	X	X	X	3	No	No	L	15
Radio Bible Class	L	X	Ind.	Ind.	No	No	X	X	X	2	X	X	L	18
Revival Fires Ministry	L	No	Ind.	Ind.	No	No	X	No**	No	1	—	No	L	10
Slavic Gospel Association	X	X	11%	Ind.	No	No	X	X	No	2	No	—	L	2
OSFO International (The T. L. Osborn Fdn.)	DID NOT RESPOND													
Tom Skinner Associates	P	X	8%	70%	No	No	X	No	No	1	Z	No	—	11
Trans-World Radio	X	X			No	X	X	X	#	1	X	X	L	2
Trinity Evangelical Divinity School	DID NOT RESPOND													
Unevangelized Fields Mission	X	X	0	50%	X	X	X	X	X	3	X	X	—	18
Underground Evangelism	X	X	100%	—	—	—	X	—	X			No	—	
Voice of China & Asia Missionary Society, Inc.	X	No	Ind.	Ind.	No	No	X	No	No	1	No	No	—	15

SECOND SURVEY

ORGANIZATION

Organization	Doctrinal Statement: Provided	Doctrinal Statement: Pre-printed	Statement of Purpose: Provided	Statement of Purpose: Pre-printed	Board List: Provided	Board List: Pre-printed	Est. % who are relatives and employees	Est. % of U.S. geography covered	Employer	Profession	Residence	Financial Statement: Provided	CPA audit	CPA letter	Complete report	No. years provided	Is latest letter unqualified?	Future Plans: Provided	Future Plans: Pre-printed	Response Time: No. of Days
World Evangelism (Morris Cerullo)	No	—	X	L	X	L	60%	Ind.	No	No	No	No	—	—	—	—	—	X	L	21
World Missionary Evangelism	X	L	X	L	No	—	—	—	—	—	No	X	X	X	X	2	X	No	—	30
World Opportunities	X	P	No	—	X	X	13%	Ind.	No	No	—	X	No	No	No	1	X	X	L	3
Youth for Christ	X	X	X	X	X	P	38%	Ind.	X	X	No	X	X	X	X	1	X	No	—	4

*An unusual problem of interpretation exists with this group. They do much overseas accounting, and they are uncommonly scrupulous in their disclosure, as is their CPA. Several other CPA letters we received called the same situation an audit. We have designated this a partial audit. (See Chapter Nine for a thorough discussion of audits and their significance.)

**Despite the GAAS/GAAP language of the letter covering this report, having only revenue and expense figures. A clean (or qualified) opinion on an incomplete report like this one is termed a piecemeal opinion, and piecemeal opinions no longer constitute acceptable auditing practice.

• CHAPTER EIGHT •

ANALYZING NON-FINANCIAL INFORMATION

Our inquiry letter, as detailed in the previous chapter, requests information in five areas. The request for financial data often yields more material, by bulk, than the other four requests combined, but this volume is not an assurance that the financial data will be the most illuminating factor for you. You can also get important information from the four non-financial requests, especially from groups that feel they have something to hide. Particularly in this dawning era of financial responsibility, accounting personnel in such organizations may spend hours grooming their financial appearance, only to have their co-workers hand you some non-financial material that undermines their carefully contrived image. The current emphasis on financial information makes the other data even more critical. For this reason we devote this chapter to a careful analysis of each of the four non-financial inquiries you can make.

We begin with the statement of purpose. This can be prime territory for the steward who relishes analyzing responses to inquiries and drawing careful conclusions from them, because it is in the statement of purpose that an organization can most accurately and meaningfully define itself — if it wants to. In this description the organization may tell you why it exists, what it is determined to accomplish, and, in broad strokes, how it is going about it. Or it may provide a statement so brief and so broad that it neither defines the goals nor the limits of its work. Part of your job is to take note of such a valueless response, and to count it against the group that provided it.

Your analysis of the statement of purpose should include two (you may say three) basic steps. First, taking everything in the statement at face value, read through it to confirm that the organization's work has enough in common with your own stewardship goals to warrant your further interest. This is your primary consideration; efficiency and effectiveness are important—but secondary. Of course, you assume you have a good idea of a group's purpose when you write to them—a purpose that triggered your initial interest. But make sure you carefully confirm that they merit your *continued* interest.

Given that confirmation, your next step is to analyze the responses to each of the other four inquiries—or, specifically, each of the inquiries to which the organization responded. (This analysis is explained in the remainder of this chapter and the next chapter.) Your final step involves reviewing the statement of purpose again, after you have reviewed everything else. But this time take nothing at face value—be critical. In the light of all the brochures and letters they've sent you and everything else you know about them, do any of the assertions in their statement of purpose now seem mere window dressing? Do they talk of a broad ministry to the whole man, but really concentrate on only the "hot button" activities that appeal so highly to the masses of donors? Do they call themselves evangelists but then fail to show you an ongoing program of evangelism? Do they talk impassionately about church planting, and raise money for church planting, but then merely reward the money to *somebody else* to plant the churches—someone they do not name, and therefore someone you cannot investigate? All in all, do they do what they *say* they do? And—when you examine all available evidence—is it obvious that they do their work *well*?

The next item you should analyze is the listing of the board of directors. To the experienced steward (and you'll get more experienced with each exchange of correspondence), this response is particularly revealing—the response that most accurately takes a "snapshot" of an organization's true character. It shows how an organization *really* views itself, in some cases contradicting the pretty picture painted in fund-raising materials—and even in some statements of purpose. Here's a prime example: many groups with supposedly significant work going on all over the world (and mass mailings reaching you regularly) can apparently recruit only the family of the top man to serve on the board. Why is this? "Why" depends on the group; either of two reasons is common. Sometimes the work of that ministry is, in fact, so ineffectual and obscure that no reputable people will associate their names with it. More often, however, these people are not being courted for positions on the board — in fact, they are being very carefully excluded because the organization is a *family business*. The people running such groups are determined to keep the affairs of their operation a totally private matter — and usually for very obvious reasons.

One organization we surveyed has a leadership comprised of three family members; they list no other board. In our first survey they sent us no financial data, but the second time they supplied us with two years' worth of audited statements. One of these listed an annual income of $7,200,000 and a $785,000 excess of revenues over expenses, two-thirds of which went unspent and became part of $1,400,000 in cash on hand. Such an accumulation of cash is not proof that the money is being misused, but it does create a problematical situation. A "good" board cannot prevent the formation of such a cash pool — but it *can* later question that formation. Eliminating this possibility is simple: no board, no questions. Although some organizations would rather maintain a reputable board and keep them at arm's length, there are still those who signal their fondness for secrecy by keeping board members "all in the family." For this reason, check the names of the board members *first* when you receive organizational information.

A much more common phenomenon than the family board is the board comprised entirely of employees of the organization — a composition that can provide similar deceptive secrecy. Both the Better Business Bureau and the Evangelical Council for Financial Accountability have established guidelines on this matter. The ECFA calls for limitation of employees and/or family members to forty-nine percent or less of the board's membership. The BBB is much more stringent, allowing no more than twenty percent. You may wonder why an organization should necessarily lose credibility for maintaining a board comprised of its own people. The answer lies in one of the board's primary functions: it is supposed to effectively represent you, the donor, as it oversees the activities of the organization. It is also supposed to see that laws governing the activities of such groups are fully obeyed, and that only the organization's stated purposes and goals are pursued. Certainly a board member would be hard pressed to effectively execute these responsibilities if he found himself opposed by a board chairman who was also his superior in the organizational hierarchy. Although a board dominated by relatives or employees is definitely a cause for suspicion, many bad choices for your support maintain boards entirely free of such taint. With this in mind, you should also scrutinize the board listing in other ways.

The board's "geographical spread" is one item to check. There should be some rough correspondence between the area of the U.S. in which an organization intends to maintain a reputation (and raise funds) and the area defined by the board members' combined communities of residence. If we find that a group headquartered in Dallas draws its board from Texas and Oklahoma almost exclusively, or that an organization in New Jersey limits board membership to people from the Middle Atlantic states, we should become leery if their outreach goes far beyond these boundaries. "Close proximity means it's much cheaper and easier to bring the board together," some say. True, but two other motives also come to mind. We can see, at the very least, a lack of interest in meaningful contact with the rest of the country. Still worse is the possibility that the board is comprised essentially of the head man's personal friends. A board drawing exclusively from the local "old boy network" is our idea of a board predictably ineffective in representing the donors' interests.

The above weaknesses are three principal warning signs that a board—and the organization behind it—may not merit your support. But besides checking for these negative factors, you should also look for encouraging signs—one of which is the variety of professions a board represents. Certainly an organization that is an association of persons of one particular profession or interest may appropriately have a board made up entirely of people chosen from among its members. For example, the Christian Medical Society is an organization of medical doctors that has a board comprised entirely of doctors. But an organization doing business with—or soliciting funds from—

the general (Christian) public should have a board composed of leaders drawn from that same general public, and that board should show variety and balance in the abilities its members bring to it. Look first for someone with strong credentials in finance and accounting. And then look for people whose talents help balance this financial strength; make sure the board isn't *overweighted* with financial talent.

As you may know, several factors operative today put financial people into more and more of the top positions in business. The current mania for conglomeration makes it impossible for corporate leaders to understand the technical skills involved in each kind of business owned by the large corporations. And the stockholders' unquenchable (and ever-increasing) thirst for growth dictates that publicly-held corporations must almost continually show growth in order to get additional capital. In fact, this growth and a "reasonable" return on investments have become the only real objectives of most large, publicly-held companies. Thus the rise of financial people. And, unfortunately, due to the tremendous influence that economic considerations have on our society, non-profit organizations traditionally think much like the profit-making ones, and often compose their boards with similar priorities.

Keep in mind that financial people tend to be quite conservative. And remember that it is possible for an organization to be so financially sound that it is of no heavenly use, to twist an old saying. For this reason, check to see that the organization is run by more than financial people; make sure that it has one or more board members who are experts in its areas of ministry. Though it is important, a group's financial soundness is not primary; their effectiveness in their ministry is of foremost importance.

The bottom line is this: make sure that you pay adequate attention to strategic information you receive about board members. It is helpful if you can get three basic pieces of information about each board member—and an organization that provides all three is certainly commendable. Because you want to determine which board members are employees and which are not; because you want to know what (if any) professional expertise each member brings to a board; and because you want to get a good idea of the geographical distribution of the board, the listing should give the following information for each member:

1. his profession, job title, or area of special capability
2. his employer or professional association
3. his state of residence

You should be skeptical of a board listing that gives only names. A list omitting one of the above three points is less than fully helpful, but probably shouldn't be downgraded.

As the summary in the previous chapter shows, twenty-nine respondents in each of our surveys supplied a board listing. Of those, eleven in the first survey and ten in the second supplied two of the three — or all three — items discussed immediately above. A final optimistic note: three groups responding to the first survey noted that they had no outside directors; by the second survey, two of the three had corrected this problem.

As you can see from these figures, however, most of the indicators in this category are negative ones. Yet much of this negative feedback gives us important information about board members. Interestingly, there really is no such thing as a negative response to the next of the four non-financial inquiries, that about future plans. Even failure to respond should not be viewed as a very negative indicator — as we have learned. In our first survey, only twenty out of the thirty-four who responded to this inquiry gave us any material; only seventeen out of thirty-one gave us information in our second survey. But we didn't interpret this negatively, because our years of experience taught us that when groups sent nothing in response, it was not because they wished to conceal their plans, but simply because they had no new projects in mind. It is often the case that parachurch ministries can grow most meaningfully simply by increasing the depth and the scope of their current work, not by developing major special projects and new goals. And we certainly want to refrain from making constant growth one of our criteria in evaluating parachurch ministries.

Nevertheless, you should interpret positively an organization's foresight if it can clearly articulate future plans. But remember that the simple presence of a statement of future plans is not a positive indicator in and of itself. You will be a better analyst — and a better steward — if you take a close look at such statements, applying two criteria: First, what do you think of the individual worth of each new project or goal described? Would this activity alone be a valuable ministry? Second, does this new activity complement and advance the group's present purposes as explained in their statement of purpose?

An example will help to illustrate this point. We don't know if China will again become a country where the gospel can be freely preached, although encouraging reports and rumors are circulating now. But the potential opportunity for evangelism in that country is so great that many organizations are already beginning to make plans to work there. Inevitably, the organizations getting ready are of two kinds: those that are qualified because they have ministered in China prior to 1949, or because they have related experience in other areas of the Orient; and those organizations drawn to the task by the fund-raising potential of such an attention-getting challenge. The wise steward will struggle to avoid being awed by plans conceived primarily to impress him.

Our final non-financial inquiry is the doctrinal statement or statement of faith. If you're interested in making useful distinctions between organizations, you will probably wait for this document with particular anticipation; unfortunately, it won't often live up to your expectations. In fact, after some experience with them, the thoughtful steward may wonder why we recommend asking for doctrinal statements at all — but we do recommend it . . . for a specific reason.

Of all those groups that will target you as a potential donor or introduce themselves to you in some manner — and then, especially among those that you, in turn, will take seriously — few will provide a doctrinal statement that will alarm you. In twenty-five years of requesting statements of this kind, we cannot recall one that did not make a traditional evangelical confession. The reason that this happens is simple: most organizations realize that the greatest percentage of people requesting doctrinal statements are evangelicals; therefore, when you ask for one, most of these groups assume that you are an evangelical.

If their statement is one that they know you would approve of, they'll send a copy to you; if not, they simply won't send it. Being "pegged" by this request will work to your advantage, because it will help you identify these organizations — and it will help them identify you. Specifically, an evangelical organization will perceive you as a strong potential donor, and a non-evangelical organization will perceive you as a much less likely donor. And most of the time this should create exactly the impression you're after.

We should make one final point about how you can practically use the doctrinal statements you obtain. Although you will seldom be able to make major distinctions among the statements you do receive, the occasions on which you do not receive such a statement will be very valuable — for this reason: because all soundly evangelical groups have adopted a statement of faith, and because most groups of other persuasions have not, you can essentially conclude that the organization failing to provide one is not evangelical — or at least not very biblical in their outlook.

When you have secured these doctrinal statements, by all means read them. Because they are practical summaries rather than theological treatises, they are brief enough to allow you to read and evaluate them quite quickly. But don't compare the contents of each statement with your own personal model of "the perfect statement" — not unless you have a very thorough understanding of theological matters. You are better off obtaining a standard doctrinal statement with which you can compare the ones you receive. It will give you a general idea of what points should be covered. We recommend one particular statement because it has been so widely adopted by soundly evangelical organizations, and because its wording has stood up to fifteen years of broad circulation and evaluation without a single change: the statement prepared and circulated by the National Association of Evangelicals. We include it below.

1. We believe the Bible to be the inspired, the only infallible, authoritative Word of God.

2. We believe that there is one God, eternally existent in three persons: Father, Son, and Holy Spirit.

3. We believe in the deity of our Lord Jesus Christ, in His virgin birth, in His sinless life, in His miracles, in His vicarious and atoning death through His shed blood, in His bodily resurrection, in His ascension to the right hand of the Father, and in His personal return in power and glory.

4. We believe that for the salvation of lost and sinful man, regeneration by the Holy Spirit is absolutely essential.

5. We believe in the present ministry of the Holy Spirit by whose indwelling the Christian is enabled to live a godly life.

6. We believe in the resurrection of both the saved and the lost; they that are saved unto the resurrection of life and they that are lost unto the resurrection of damnation.

7. We believe in the spiritual unity of believers in our Lord Jesus Christ.

• CHAPTER NINE •

ANALYZING FINANCIAL INFORMATION

Accounting, when practiced as a science — or as an art — is a very complicated matter. But this chapter is meant only to clarify some standard accounting practices for the layman. It is *not* written for the Certified Public Accountant, but for the man and woman in the pew — for you. It will not enable you to complete a detailed financial analysis of any annual report sent your way. But it will give you a few basic analytical tests that you can apply to a statement to determine, in a simple and basic way, an organization's financial soundness.

At the outset you should realize what a financial report is — and what it isn't. Financial statements tell you how much money an organization received and, more or less, how it was spent. In general, financial information offers you a valuable clue about how careful an organization is with its money. Remember, though, that these reports offer no information about how effectively the organization executes its ministry. Probably because financial information is so quantitative, so precise in this scientific age, we tend to overvalue it, and to confuse this measuring of efficiency with one of effectiveness. We should be determined not to make this mistake.

When you look at a financial statement for the first time, you may feel discouraged, not knowing where to begin. But, happily, there is a right place to start. You should first check for the two most important virtues in financial reporting: accuracy and year-to-year consistency. Because these qualities are so vital, our society values them very highly, and, through government and the business community, it has taken measures to insist on them.

Thus the financial reports of corporations that are publicly owned (those that issue stock to the public) *must* be audited annually; and this audit must be performed by a Certified Public Accountant whose right to practice is extended to him by his state government through certification. Though only publicly-held companies are required to submit to an audit, our society is so thoroughly convinced of the basic value of this procedure that a majority of all reputable organizations (both profit and non-profit) are voluntarily audited every year by a CPA firm.

This, then, is your starting place, the first point to notice about any annual report you are reviewing: Has it been audited by a CPA? Because of the importance of this question, it is essential that you answer it carefully. Do not assume that an annual report has been audited by a CPA, regardless of its apparent authenticity; you must have the auditing CPA's written word for it. Specifically, the CPA is obliged by professional requirements to accompany a financial report he has audited with a written opinion, in letter form, attesting to his use of "generally accepted auditing standards," and to the "fairness" of the statement in relation to "generally accepted accounting principles." (In the professional jargon of accountants this is called a GAAS/GAAP opinion.) Without the letter you cannot be sure that you have an audited statement, because it is only the CPA's attestation in the signed letter that confirms this.

Logically enough, it is standard procedure for the audited organization to include this letter when sending their annual report to anyone. In fact, organizations that publish their annual report in printed form invariably include the CPA's letter as one of the accompanying pages of the report. The CPA gives one of three possible opinions in his letter: unqualified ("clear"), qualified, and adverse. An adverse opinion states that the documents examined "do not present fairly the financial position of the organization." Few groups ever get an adverse opinion, and none would ever circulate one. You are almost certainly not going to get one from an inquiry. A "clean" opinion is the CPA's unqualified attestation that "the documents examined present fairly the financial position of the organization." As a rule of thumb, you might say that "the shorter the letter, the cleaner the opinion," though this certainly isn't a professional criterion for judgment. Here is an example of the contents of a clean opinion letter:

In our opinion, the accompanying statement of financial position and the related statements of income and expenses and changes in fund balances present fairly the financial position of XYZ Ministry at December 31, 19X2 and 19X1, and the results of this organization's operations for the year then ended, in conformity with generally accepted accounting principles consistently applied.

Our examinations of these statements were made in accordance with generally accepted auditing standards and such other auditing procedures as we considered necessary under the circumstances.

A qualified letter is the most difficult type to judge. It attests to a fair presentation, but gives only qualified and limited approval. Overseas accounting is a particularly difficult matter that makes a significant qualification necessary.[1] The reason why is simple to determine: Most foreign mission organizations do not undergo the rigor (and the cost) of extending the accounting procedures of their home office to their various field offices, nor the further effort of then combining financial statements of operations around the world into a single statement, and submitting it for audit. When, in such circumstances, the auditor is asked to review only the U. S. figures, he usually issues a qualified opinion citing the circumstances — unless he declines to express an opinion at all. For organizations whose very reason for being is their overseas operations, this is not a minor qualification. Not surprisingly, the matter of overseas audit is a highly debatable issue for the Accounting Task Force of the IFMA, because the significant cost of doing this overseas accounting must be weighed against the value of the result.

On the other hand, however, a qualified opinion is often given for quite a minor reason, as this sample paragraph from a CPA's cover letter shows:

In November 19X1, the Financial Accounting Standards Board issued new standards of financial accounting and reporting for lease agreements and, accordingly, as described

---

[1]CPA's strongly disagree about the best professional way to handle the problem of overseas accounting. Some said they would give an unqualified opinion in this case; others would refuse to express an opinion at all.

in Note 3 to the financial statements, the organization, during the fiscal year ended March 31, 19X2, changed its method of accounting for certain leases to comply with the new accounting standards.

You probably shouldn't interpret a letter like this one as an indictment. Certainly "qualified opinion" letters must be carefully evaluated, but don't let any qualifications, whether major or minor, obscure the central fact — the fact that *the letter does attest to an audit*. The organization with a qualified letter is certainly in much better standing with us — having submitted to the audit and sent the letter — than are those who refused to be audited, to say nothing of those who refused us financial information of any sort.

But, even though a CPA's opinion is important, remember that it is not the perfect safeguard: CPA's are fallible, too. A primary problem develops because many CPA firms are small; in fact, often a single person *is* the firm. They often need (Christian) organizations as clients more than the clients need them. To preserve these relationships, they are sometimes less honest than they should be — behavior that is not hard to understand when we look at the circumstances.

The major accounting firms (the top number are commonly called "The Big Eight") are almost always involved strictly with audits: they audit the work of accountants who are full-time employees in the (usually huge) organizations they have as clients. But the smaller CPA firms do most of their business as internal accountants, going into small organizations and pulling together the financial records at the end of the fiscal year. This is a much larger job than simply performing an audit, and it is an important piece of business to a small firm. Having straightened out the records for the year, and done the end-of-year statement, the CPA finds it a simple matter to audit his own work, so he frequently offers his professional opinion at little additional charge. This is a nice arrangement for both parties: the CPA gets a good chunk of work, and the client gets an audit and the added bonus of a clean — or at worst, mildly qualified — opinion letter. Nevertheless, you should be wary of this seemingly congenial situation — as our survey proves. Regrettably, we discovered two problems caused by such a situation, both of which we describe below:

1. Consider this hypothetical case: The CPA has worked for several days at an organization, putting together the year's financial records. However, under client orders, he has prepared the annual statement in such a way that it could never clear an audit. For this reason he doesn't perform an audit, and he doesn't render an opinion, and he explains all this clearly in his letter — on his CPA stationery. He is technically innocent, because none of his work requires his certification. In this case the organization plays the heavy, because it hopes to use the letter to lull you, the inquirer, into a non-judgmental sleep.

If this seems like an overly strong statement, consider an actual response we received. The letter from the ministry thanks us for our inquiry, and then states, "Please find enclosed the following: . . . the financial statement for [last] year, including a copy of the auditor's cover letter." Then, apparently wanting to bolster our confidence in the report, the respondent adds, ". . . We want you to feel free to contact the auditor who did the work for us. He is a fine Christian gentleman and has been a real help to us." But, lo and behold, the auditor's cover letter says, in its entirety:

> The accompanying balance sheet as of December 31, the related statement of activity, and the supplementary schedule (Schedules 1 through 18) have been prepared from the accounts of the organization. We have not audited these financial statements and, therefore, express no opinion on them.

You may note that the sixty-five responses to our survey yielded forty-five cover letters from CPA's but only forty audits. These results support our earlier-mentioned caution: *Don't assume that a letter indicates an audit.* Read the letter to ensure that it says what you think it does.

2. Another respondent in our survey is large for a parachurch organization, especially considering the small size of its CPA firm. Essentially, this group is beyond reproach, even exemplary. But, like many well-established organizations

that are used to the "old rules" of financial privacy, they seem to be having a hard time adjusting to financial disclosure. Perhaps their reluctance is triggered by their substantial assets and cash reserves, which they don't want the layman to misinterpret. In any case, in our first survey they didn't send us a complete financial report; they sent us a CPA letter (drawn up by a small firm) and a single document that detailed expenses.

What troubles us is that the CPA noted in his cover letter that he audited the total statement—but not all portions of the statement were included with the letter. This exclusion is a violation of professional auditing standards: the CPA cannot mention that he audited parts of the statement and then not include them. He is also responsible for carefully controlling the distribution of reports covered by his letters to prevent organizations from excluding this information. Unfortunately, though the organization itself is principally to blame, it is the CPA whom the accounting community would hold responsible if this case were discovered.

Not surprisingly, the larger, more established CPA firms protect their valuable reputations by carefully ensuring that the client circulates exactly what was audited—nothing less. We wonder if the CPA mentioned above took his cue from them— if he pressured his client to stop distributing his letter without complete financial statements—because his letter did not accompany the response to our second survey. What we received was a bareboned financial report (not a complete one) and a letter that, because of wording and format, appeared to be an audit cover letter. But on closer inspection we realized that it wasn't the genuine article: it refers to an audit cover letter, and attests that such a letter was written, but it is not such a letter. This letter probably clears the CPA with the State Board of Accountancy, but we think the organization is culpable in this instance, because it appears that this letter was used to deceive. Fortunately, we can end this discussion on a positive note: the ECFA (to which this ministry belongs) requested detailed information about this situation, and received it. We're hoping that this exploration has a constructive outcome.

By recounting this incident, we do not mean to imply that

a small CPA firm is necessarily a victim of its size; its strength
and the quality of its work depend on its employees. But we
do contend that the nature of the relationship between a small
CPA firm and a larger client sometimes makes the CPA too
willing to please, and the client too willing to take advantage
of the situation.

As a fair and responsible steward, you don't want to draw
the wrong conclusions from this illustration and become overly
suspicious. But you should handle the issue of disclosure real-
istically and effectively. This means routinely checking organizational responses to make sure that correct disclosure
procedures have been followed. And you should be on your
guard when you get a CPA cover letter that does not begin by
listing the documents the CPA examined in the audit — or when
you do not receive all of the documents cited in the CPA's
letter. If either of these shortcomings is evident, and if the
pages of the report you receive are photocopied (suggesting
that it is not one of the CPA's originals and might be sent
without his acknowledgment), you should have some reserva-
tions about the organization in question. Also, be on the alert
for the statement covered by a CPA audit letter but not comprising what we define later in this chapter as a "complete
report."

When your analysis indicates (as the instances above do)
that it is the client who is taking liberties (you can never be
sure that the CPA involved knows these things are happening),
contact the organization, telling them what information you
received and what information you didn't get. Next, get in
touch with the Society of Certified Public Accountants in your
state and have them determine if the report you received is
standard (OK) or substandard. If they think what you have is
substandard, forward copies to your State Board of Accountancy. (You can find the addresses of both of these offices in
the phone book.) Finally, contact the accounting establishment
itself.

We urge you to go to such lengths not only so that you
can give wisely, but so that you can discourage organizations
from withholding information — particularly those reputable
organizations that only hurt themselves by doing so. Let us

inspire you with a few examples of what unaudited data can be like. During our surveys we received financial information from one ministry that consisted of just a single page of photocopy briefly listing expenses for the past year. Another unaudited report listed seventy percent of total revenue as "other income," with no breakdown or explanation. The same report listed sixty percent of expenses as "other costs." And in this instance, the source is a well-known and deeply committed ministry.[2] In our opinion, such material is an insult to the steward receiving it. And when we consider these refusals of sufficient disclosure, at the same time recognizing the possibility of outright fraud by the simple use of fictitious numbers, we realize how vulnerable we are when we accept unaudited data. For this reason we believe that every steward requesting financial information must face the complex challenge of how to treat unaudited reports.

True, the audit is not a sure solution, not a panacea in this situation. Some unaudited statements we have received provide greater detail and more helpful explanatory notes than do many audited statements; and some audited statements are amazingly brief. Nevertheless, we must admit this to ourselves: we usually trust a brief audited statement sooner than we trust a more complete unaudited statement. In those few instances that we're comfortable with unaudited statements, we usually know the organizations well enough that we don't really think it's necessary to consult their financial information. But what it really comes down to is this: You, the steward — and only you — must decide how you will regard unaudited reports. You may decide case by case, or you may make an across-the-board, once-and-for-all decision. Either way, we encourage you to be prepared, because we are sure that — at least in the near future — inquirers will continue to receive many unaudited statements.

At present, the principal problem is this: many organizations still hesitate to give audited financial reports to "the great unwashed" — the donors. Ironically, they do not hesitate to submit their audited statements to the IFMA or ECFA — both of which require audits of all their members. In fact, the majority

---

[2] We are happy to report that this ministry supplied us with complete and audited financial information in our second survey.

of these groups are fund-raising leaders and have been audited for years. These organizations simply need to recognize the public's need to know — and to recognize the primary purpose of the IFMA and the ECFA: not to accumulate vast files of audited financial statements, but rather to bring about the day when every organization soliciting funds for evangelical purposes is obliged to furnish this information to any inquirer.

Although the ECFA and the IFMA Task Force may, at the outset, have trouble enforcing the audit requirement, it nevertheless seems likely that in the not-too-distant future any worthy evangelical organization will feel obliged to belong to a group that requires audits as a matter of course. Certainly the mere founding of these two associations has opened numerous doors previously closed to the inquiring steward. In fact, our survey turned up evidence of progress almost certainly triggered by these two groups. Our first survey produced seventeen audited statements; our second produced twenty-two such statements. Even though the apparent gain is only five, actually eight organizations that refused us financial information, ignored our request for it, or weren't audited the first time gave us at least one year's audited data in the second survey. (Three groups that gave information the first time failed to respond to the second survey.) We are thankful to God for this preliminary indication of change. But until this change is complete, the inquiring steward will continue to receive unaudited statements and will have to decide what to do with them: whether to accept, analyze, and believe them — or ignore them.

When you do receive a response with a CPA's cover letter attesting to an audit and rendering an opinion, what should you look for next? Check first of all for a "complete report." This is the detailed financial statement that the auditor must have in order to apply whatever accounting tests he thinks are necessary. For organizations of the type we are dealing with, auditing procedures dictate that a complete report consists of these four units of information:[3]

---

[3] *A summary of changes in financial position* is an optional unit of information that indicates an organization's willingness to exhaustively disclose financial data.

1. A *balance sheet*, listing all assets and liabilities and fund balances.

An *"activity report"* consisting of the following:
2. a listing, by category, of all revenues for the fiscal year;
3. a listing, by category, of all expenses for the fiscal year; and
4. a summary of changes in fund balances since the same date last year.

It is also the auditor's responsibility to require that his client's financial statement contain sufficient notes of explanation. These notes should explain how the accountant handled various problems that arose in preparing the statement. They should also explain which of several accounting procedures were chosen at specific points in the preparation of the statement.

When you begin drawing conclusions from the figures themselves, we advise that you keep your investigative ambitions within sensible bounds. We suggest that you attempt to make only three observations and conclusions from the data proper. Assuming you are working with a "complete report," we think you should be able to do the following:

1. Learn whether or not the organization in question spent — within the scope of its ministry — all or most of what it received. If not, what was done with the unspent remainder?

2. Determine the ratio between revenues and other funds applied to ministry, and those funds used to sustain the organization itself.

3. Quickly assess the financial health of the organization. Do they have sufficient liquid (cash or readily cashable) assets to cover their short-term liabilities?

Below we flesh out these three points of analysis, doing so with the confidence that they can be used to draw reliable conclusions about an organization. None of the three is difficult to derive from a properly presented annual report.

Revenue vs. Expense

Locate the three elements of what we term the *activity report* — statements of revenues, of expenses, and of changes in fund balances for the period. Not all organizations use a format that lists these items together, but revenues and expenses are rarely listed far apart and are usually easy to find. After quickly perusing the two categories, note the totals for each, checking to see if there is an excess of revenue or a deficit. If you notice a deficit, look for evidence suggesting how the deficit is being met. Significant borrowing from restricted funds for more than one year should warn you of financial weakness. While you're scrutinizing the report, see if the summary of changes in fund balances gives a separate listing of restricted funds (such as annuity payments received). Also notice what details it provides about these funds, keeping in mind that *long-term* details are what you need. A single year of revenue deficit doesn't reveal much; that's why having three years' worth of reports is so important. Unfortunately, this information isn't always easy to get. In our first survey, only eleven out of twenty-eight financial respondents (audited and unaudited) sent us three years' information. In our second survey the proportion was even lower: only nine out of thirty organizations gave us what we aked for. Nevertheless, be persistent. This information is worth working for and will probably become increasingly easy to secure.

Besides watching for deficits, be on the lookout for excess of revenue over expense. You should attempt to follow that excess through the report to see what happened to it. Some reports will indicate where the money went immediately below the excess figure. Others will show it as a source of working capital. When the latter procedure is followed, see how much of that increase went into capital outlay during the period, and how much went to a net increase in working capital, to be carried over as such. This should show up in the statement of changes in financial position, if one is provided. A year-after-year excess in revenue over expenditure and a year-after-year net increase in working capital are not encouraging signs. What accounts for the big build-up? Is the organization preparing for a major increase in effort—or simply lining its own pockets?

But a much more serious red flag should appear when that excess "disappears" and can't be traced through the report, because our main objective in this first test is to spot significant excess revenue, and to find out what is being done with it.

Program vs. Support

The steward's job in this next test is to determine which expenditures have gone to sustain the organization's ministries, and which have gone to sustain the organization itself. Many people in non-profit circles stress the importance of determining how much was spent on fund-raising. But we think this quest can be somewhat misguided if it diminishes concern for the size of other administrative costs. Much more helpful (and reliable) for appraisal purposes is a quantitative indicator of the amount that a non-profit group does not spend on its ministry. The IFMA's *Accounting & Financial Reporting Guide*[4] uses the term *program services* for all funds spent on ministry, and the term *support services* for all funds spent on organizational maintenance. The job here is to take the entries under expenditures and classify each as program or support — although some annual reports will do this for you. Naturally, the more detail available in the report, the more accurate your breakdown will be. The IFMA Guide devotes an entire chapter (Chapter 6) to this classification of program and support services. Although this guide is primarily intended to help organizations prepare statements, it is still very helpful reading for stewards analyzing financial information.

When you have classified every item, sometimes appropriately dividing an item between the two columns (a procedure that the IFMA Guide explains), add up both the program and service columns. Finally, divide the program figure by the service figure to obtain a ratio of the two categories of expenditure. According to guidelines commonly followed by groups whose business it is to arbitrate such things, your ratio should come out at 3.0 or higher — i.e., support services should constitute no more than twenty-five percent of total expenditures.[5] When you use this indicator, keep two things in mind. First, remember the importance of consistency. When an annual report yields a ratio under 3.0 for the most recent fiscal year, be sure to develop the ratio for the two previous years, also; the *average*

[4]This guide is available for $11.00 from the IFMA, Box 395, Wheaton, IL, 60187.
[5]Use of this ratio is not appropriate for educational institutions.

ratio is the key factor. Second, understand that the ratio is intended as a guideline. A ratio of 2.9 or lower may be acceptable if there's a good explanation for it — if it represents a problem that the group is working to overcome and willing to discuss with you. If you are seriously interested in their work, don't hesitate to ask.

Assets vs. Liabilities

You can get a general picture of the financial health of an organization by comparing their current assets with their current liabilities. These figures appear prominently on a *balance sheet* as the upper portions of the assets and liabilities sections. If current liabilities outweigh current assets, don't automatically sound the death knell, because it is possible that contributions from a loyal constituency would continue to flow in — possibly even increasing in number — and eliminate such a financial squeeze. Nevertheless, such a possibility shouldn't strongly influence your analysis of the financial report. The balance sheet is a financial "snapshot" of the organization at a particular time (the last day of the fiscal year), and the essential consideration is this: If the group has no more money than the amount shown, does it have the reserves to meet its current obligations? But keep in mind that often the source of the needed cash lies just below the total current assets line in an item entitled something like "Long-term Investments." If these investments — or at least the portion necessary to meet cash demands — are in marketable securities, they are, for all purposes, as good as cash. The notes to the financial statements should explain the "liquidity factor" of such assets.

When this added source of cash is not available, an organization with current liabilities in excess of current assets would be obliged to borrow, to sell something not readily marketable, or to seriously change in some other way its pattern of operation if current obligations came due. Such weakness constitutes the lack of financial health that this third test is designed to uncover. Certainly its presence must be counted heavily against the organization in question.

After you perform these three financial tests, you should have a fairly adequate picture of the basic financial status of an organization. These tests are easy to perform, and they don't emphasize financial considerations over non-financial ones.

As we conclude this discussion, we cannot help but think of the obligations we have placed on you, our reader. We ask a lot of you in this book. If you follow our suggestions, you will not only be a well-informed steward — you will be a very busy one. You have to be quite committed to your stewardship responsibilities to aggressively undertake some or all of the steps we recommend. Again we emphasize that our approach is not systematic or holistic, and that these procedures are not so interrelated that one won't work without the others. Nevertheless, we ask a lot of you.

Now, having admitted that we're asking a lot, we want to ask one more thing of you. Let the end of this discussion be only the beginning of your use of this book. Begin immediately to take those steps that you think will strengthen your stewardship. Begin immediately to verify the value of the work being done by those you are supporting — or to seek out other, more worthy recipients. And work — work prayerfully at your stewardship. Give every dollar carefully. Remember that your individual work as a steward is absolutely essential to the larger work of the Great Commission.